ETERNAL ROSE

A Novel

Timothy J. Hatton

Hog Press

Hog Press
an imprint of Culicidae Press®
PO Box 5069
Madison, WI 53705-5069
hogpress.com
editor@hogpress.com

Hog Press

ETERNAL ROSE, A NOVEL
Copyright © 2025 by Timothy J. Hatton
All rights reserved.

No part of this book may be reproduced in any form by any electronic or mechanized means (including photocopying, recording, or information storage and retrieval) without written permission, except in the case of brief quotations embodied in critical articles and reviews. For more information, please visit culicidaepress.com

ISBN: 978-1-68315-112-8

Our books may be purchased in bulk for promotional, educational or business use. Please contact your local bookseller or the Culicidae Press Sales Department at +1-352-215-7558 or by email at sales@culicidaepress.com

culicidaepress.bsky.social – facebook.com/culicidaepress
threads.net/@culicidaepress – instagram.com/culicidaepress
x.com/culicidaepress

Design by polytekton © 2025
Cover image generated by Midjourney AI system and modified by polytekton

I dedicate this book first to Jesus Christ and to my family and friends who believed in me. I know that if there was no You, there would be no Me!
Thank you!

TABLE OF CONTENTS

Part I	**6**
Chapter 1	6
Chapter 2	11
Chapter 3	16
Chapter 4	29
Chapter 5	34
Chapter 6	37
Part II	**58**
Chapter 7	58
Chapter 8	64
Chapter 9	69
Chapter 10	73
Chapter 11	77
Chapter 12	84
Chapter 13	88
Chapter 14	91
Chapter 15	94
Chapter 16	99
Chapter 17	104
Chapter 18	111
Chapter 19	122

Part III   **129**
    Chapter 20   129
    Chapter 21   132
    Chapter 22   136
    Chapter 23   140
    Chapter 24   145
    Chapter 25   152
    Chapter 26   154
    Chapter 27   160

Part IV   **170**
    Chapter 28   170
    Chapter 29   173
    Chapter 30   177
    Chapter 31   182
    Chapter 32   186
    Chapter 33   192
    Chapter 34   196
    Chapter 35   200
    Chapter 36   207

Part V   **212**
    Chapter 37   212
    Chapter 38   216
    Chapter 39   222
    Chapter 40   224
    Chapter 41   230

Part I

Chapter 1

"Bury the past or the past will bury you!" a quote given to ten-year-old Connie Casson by her father who never seemed to bury anything, especially old grudges!

She knew her father could be very mean or very nice and he seldom took his own advice. "Bury the past or the past will bury you!" Oh, how she longed for him to do just that; instead, her father would ruminate on things for hours, days, months, and even years. He would, as she often put it to the few friends she had, "blow up like an overfilled basketball just waiting to pop," and she knew today was one of those days.

With eyes full of regret and remembrance Connie sat rather quietly on an old soft bottom rocker watching her drunken father stumble toward her mother who was sleeping rather peacefully on an old rusty wrought iron frame bed and cocooned in a ratty old red and white quilt with her right arm lying on a gingham covered pillow with a brand new cast with the words, "I love you, Mommie" written on it.

"Marthee, oh how I love thee, yep — yep" her father sang out — dribbling fresh vomit down his grey threadbare suit, hiding a bear of a man, filthy, smelly and dangerous. "Dad, please leave Mommie alone — just go sleep it off" Connie blurted out as she jumped up in front of him wearing old rose-colored pajamas torn, but clean. She hated when her father acted this way. It never ended well. A sharp pain shot deep inside her as if somehow tonight things were going to be really bad. She felt this time her father was really, really drunk and out of control.

Her father, who had at one time been highly esteemed, now pushed her aside like she meant nothing to him, and he started to sing again. "Oh Marthee, love me. I just want a little lovin', that's all." He returned, burping and vomiting some more, unaware as it slid down his three-month-old beard. "No! Leave her alone, she just got out of the hospital yesterday. Oh, how I hate you when you" — and without warning her father swooped down and grabbed her by the arms and pulled her up to his level and, with breath as bad as an outhouse in August, he screamed, "Don't you ever say you hate me again! You got that? I'm your father, I made you, you got that? Without me you're nothin'. Oh, why do I even bother with you? You're a worthless piece of crap." Then, without warning he slapped her, then dropped her on the old, scarred hardwood floor, causing her to land hard on her bottom as she burst into tears.

"Martha, Martha love me," Connie's father blurted out again as he headed for his wife who was still sleeping through all the commotion. Connie vaulted toward her father and grabbed him from behind, stopping his progress. "No, Daddy, leave her alone, please! Don't hurt her, don't!"

"Shut up! I'm not gonna hurt her. I just want some lovin', that's all."

"No, please leave her alone, please!" Connie pleaded as she tried to tackle her father. As she grabbed him around his ankles, revealing mismatched shoes and no socks, he started to fall.

"That's it! Let me go! You've been a curse since the day you were born" he blurted back. Catching himself, he snatched her up and threw her across an old grey and black sea chest at the foot of the bed, causing her to smack her head severely.

Her mother finally stirred, sat up and looked around as if she was still dreaming. She saw the old black and white photos in antique frames on the wall, covered in dust, of parents and cousins. It seemed her reverie was more real than her present life and, as if coming out of nowhere, lightning flashed and a thought illuminated deep within her that perhaps a real storm was headed her way, one that she just might not recover from. Thunder shook the small cheap apartment causing her to fully awaken. She heard her daughter crying, rubbing her head. That was it! She started yelling, "What have you done to Connie? I said if you touch her or me again, we're outta here! I meant it!"

Connie's mother jumped off the bed and with her good arm, grabbed Connie and headed for the door held on with one hinge. "You can't go anywhere!" Connie's father shot back, grabbing her mother's good arm and squeezing it. I won't let you go! Besides, lightning turns me on! Come on Martha, a little lovin'. You know I didn't do nothin' to Connie. She's just clumsy, that's all. She tripped."

"Let go of me! You want to break my good arm too?" Connie's mother yelled, moving quickly from the bedroom to the kitchen, holding Connie tightly by her side. As she entered the kitchen, with Connie hanging onto her black moo-moo, the lights flickered, revealing a thousand roaches each bigger than a man's thumb, a black and silver plastic table set, and a dirty Formica counter with half open cans of green beans and corn, as if someone wanted to eat them, but had changed their mind, along with a half empty pint of cheap liquor and a liver-cheese sandwich with a small jar of mayonnaise and a very large butcher knife beside it, much too big for the job. For some reason, a bad feeling shot through her. She yelled, "Connie, go outside!" Run outside now!" Her husband caught her from behind and said rather softly, "Come on." He tried to spin his wife around and kiss her, but she wouldn't consent. With a boldness that had been simmering, seemingly for the last twenty years, she pushed her husband away, causing him to lose his balance. She yelled again, "Enough! I've taken enough! I don't love you anymore! You're a poor excuse for a man. You beat me, you cuss at me, you hurt our own child; the one we asked God for. Honestly, I really did love you at one time but look what you've become. I never thought I'd ever say this, but I don't want to ever see you again!" Connie's mother said, bursting into tears. Lightning flashed again as thunder rumbled the entire neighborhood. She watched as her husband's face grew expressionless for a moment, as if he was soaking in what she said, as if something was resonating inside him. It was as if he was finally realizing how much he had hurt his family through the years. He looked around at the dirty sink full of dishes, the metal cabinets with doors hanging off the hinges, the cheap cups and the no-name silverware, the dirty linoleum floor, the dead rats, the holes knocked in the plaster walls, (from, as he declared, minor disagreements). He wondered, "How could things have gotten so bad?" He had been a tenured professor, and he had now become a derelict; all because of one dumbfounded accusation. As he watched his wife head for the door, it seemed they were really going to leave this time. The reality suddenly cut deep into his heart, and he suddenly grew angry. His face tightened and he grabbed his wife, holding her like a clamp. "No one walks out on Jack Casson! No one! Martha, you're my woman. I own you! I made you! No other man would want you anyway. You're old, fat and ugly and your daughter is as homely as you."

"Let go of me now! I'm done! Connie, Run! Run!" Connie's mother screamed, breaking away, (why she paused only she could answer. Maybe she hoped he would transform back into the man she fell in love with during her senior year of high school.)

"I can't let you go! If I can't have you, no man ever will," Connie's father said through clenched teeth. Without thinking, he reached over to the counter and grabbed the butcher knife with the mayonnaise still on it and started to stab his wife over and over again. Blood gushed out everywhere as he ignored the screams of his daughter, "No, Daddy please! Please don't! NO!"

Connie watched her mother slump down into a pool of her own blood. She grabbed her mother when the stabbing ended and with her last breath her mother gurgled, "I love you," then she closed her eyes for the last time, just as lightning flashed again.

Chapter 2

Fifty years later and a world away, the lightning flashed again as Constance Magenta mumbled, "Stop, stop stabbing her! Mommie, Mommie, I love you. No, no, don't die. No."

Shaking her head as she mumbled, trying to rid herself of that horrible image, she got up from her huge custom crafted four poster bed made of cherry wood, her favorite. She sat quietly on the edge of her bed, still curled up in purple, pink and white luxury linens. Finally, pulling the covers back, she went over to her large vanity that was shaped like a giant heart with lights all around the heart. She sat down and by memory turned on a ballerina shaped lamp. When the light came on, she noticed all of her makeup; lip gloss, eyelash case, eyeliner and various creams, many designed just for her skin type, which was a light golden color, mostly free from splotches, liver spots and veins. She tried to keep herself looking good even though she was getting close to sixty now.

She sighed again as she lingered at her vanity, just as a flash of lightning lit up the whole massive bedroom adorned with renowned crystal lamps. The dressers and nightstands, which had been gathered from antique galleries and auctions from Florida to Paris, were her most prized antiques and furnishings designed by her favorite French designer. She adored her two palm-frond monkey-motif floor lamps. All of her drapes were covered in splendid colors of dark red. Constance stared at herself in the mirror. She picked at an imaginary blemish, which she did often. She stared deeper into the image, perhaps wishing she could be someone else. "Cinderella, no," she thought to herself. I'm already that; besides, I would have to dress up in stomachers and tippets — not me" she said.

She paused in her reflection, and the horrible dream that fluttered through her mind once again like some mayfly toward a streetlight. She continued talking to herself as she watched her small thin lips move in the mirror. "How come I'm not happy? I have everything. Yet I have nothing. My mother is dead; my father has been locked away in Fulton for years and, yes, what about my good old father? If he'd only known what his actions did to my life that day, an only child. I spent years in the foster care systems. Some were good, some simply a nightmare." She paused briefly as an image came to her of her first foster care home where she was spanked harshly for taking another apple because she was still hungry. Or the time she regurgitated and was forced to do the unthinkable, because her foster mom said it was done just to criticize her cooking. She tried to rid herself of that episode of her life. Then she continued talking to herself, "Father, you don't realize the times I had to fight off overhormoned foster kids or other people who thought I was an easy mark. Or, Father, you don't realize all the times I saw you stabbing mother over and over again in my dreams. And my crying and praying to God that it was all just a bad dream and that, somehow, we'd just all eat dried toast and Cream o' Wheat in the morning, and that everything would be right with the world again. Don't you get it Father? I cried my eyes out night after night. I'm so glad that God says He keeps our tears in a bottle and records them in a book in heaven. I bet you — I have a million bottles up there. You know, I heard they let you out after forty years, and that's been over ten years ago. I want to see you, but yet, I don't. It was you that took my precious mother, my best friend away from me. Yes God, I'm trying to forgive. But it sure isn't easy."

"Well, I really need to stop talking about all this. I'm liable to get depressed. Maybe I need to think about something else, yes, something else, what about my Charleton, my wonderful husband, he's not home again. When he is home, he hardly talks to me. He never discusses anything until after the fact. It's as if he thinks I'm too stupid to understand his world. Why, I used to keep the books for him when he was building decks and putting up fences. But now, since he's a big shot or thinks he is, anyway, because he builds highways, bridges, skyscrapers, and mega-malls, suddenly I'm a lamebrain."

"Yes, it does irritate me that he just goes around me like I was invisible and does things. Like now, he's going to tell the world some great news tonight. You'd think he'd discuss it with me first, his supposedly best friend, but no, not me. I think his money is his best friend. I can't remember the last time he looked deep into my eyes and told me he loved me more than anything in the whole world and that I was his treasure, his pearl. You know a woman really needs to hear that."

"I mean, I keep myself fit. I always wear the perfume he prefers. I always dress nice, I make sure the home is kept, but I still get no passion. Oh yes, there are times we enjoy each other, but not nearly enough for me. I'm a woman! I need to be loved, to be talked to, to be comforted. I do get tired of hugging his pillow. Now there, there Constance, you must be more like the 'Brits' and keep a stiff upper lip. You're now a member of the fabulously wealthy according to "Forbes." Enough already."

Constance stopped talking to herself. She pursed her lips, got up and glanced over to her husband's side of the bed and said aloud, dropping back into melancholy, "Oh Charleton, Charleton, must you always be gone, trying to be the king of the world? Can't you just stay home with me and hold me, please? I really want to be held, just to be loved. Oh, Charleton, please."

Constance turned briefly back to the mirror and smiled. She was dressed in a pink silk monogrammed nightgown. She knew at her age she was still quite beautiful. Her long brunette hair which had been longer was now just past her shoulders. She had long ago decided that real long hair was just for schoolgirls, and not for women past their prime. Her eyes were brown and set deep into her face, with perfect cheekbones. She could have done runway in her younger years. Her lips were perfectly matched, her commissure made them so inviting. She was five foot eight inches tall in heels, which she wore all the time, and one hundred and ten pounds (she always felt a hundred and five was just right for her). And whenever she gained more than five pounds, she would increase her workout at her home gym three to five times a week using a personal trainer she had on call. Her gym with its bow flex, weights, stationary bike, Stairmaster and a Jacuzzi to comfort her sore muscles, all wrapped up with a trip to Merle Norman and Frederick's, her favorite hair salon, which made her feel like a new woman.

As she thought about her outward beauty, she knew inside she didn't feel beautiful at all. She just couldn't understand why. She knew she had every material thing a woman could ever want. She lived in a huge mansion on Old Highway 63 south of Columbia, Missouri on 300 acres. The mansion was designed after an old-world provincial style with the romance of the French Riviera. It was a full two stories with each room having their own balcony upstairs, built of blonde brick with eight fireplaces, six bedrooms and six bathrooms.

The estate had large arching windows and two huge picture windows with hedges underneath them, one in the living room, and the other in the so-called Great Room which was one thousand feet wide by twelve hundred feet long, and it could easily seat five hundred guests. It had a sculptured wood ceiling with Baccarat chandeliers which reflected handsomely on the polished wood floor, and in the large mirror that rose to the ceiling above the eight-feet-by-six-feet-wide marble fireplace.

Constance thought about the marble columns and the marble steps and porch with lions crouching on the end of the marble banisters. The swimming pool, the fine manicured lawns and her flower garden (she smiled when she thought about this) added life to her. She had never had a "green thumb," but as a hobby she took up planting roses, pansies, violets, and tulips. The act of watching something grow from the ground up seemed to add something wonderful, as she put it, to her mostly dull life. Presently it seemed to be the only thing that made her smile other than an occasional trip around the world to obtain an antique piece she had wanted for years. Even though these allowed a brief respite between her loneliness, she knew deep down inside she needed more. There seemed to be a real ache inside of her, an itching that she just couldn't satisfy.

Constance, now more than anything, wanted to be happy — really happy like a child on Christmas morning or a new bride. She wanted a happiness that would last for a lifetime, not just for a moment. She sat down on the edge of her bed, growing a little weary of all her continual musings over what she did and didn't have in her life.

She turned and looked at her pillow and blankets and wanted to get back in bed, cover her head up and forget the rest of her life. But without even realizing she'd set the alarm clock, it went off. She looked at it and said, "Oh brother, six am already," just as lightning flashed again and thunder shook her home.

CHAPTER 3

"Mrs. M," Frances, the head maid, said, looking through Constance's open bedroom door of heavy sculptured cherry, through which Constance was about to exit. Frances said it again, "Mrs. M." (She always called her that for reasons only she understood; her last name was Magenta, which didn't seem difficult for anyone else.)

Frances was as skinny as a rake handle. She wore a black blouse and skirt with white lace from her neck to her knees. She had a white tiara in her auburn hair, and she smiled a lot, but her teeth were too small for her gums which made her look like a little girl. An excellent worker, a great cook, but a little nosy, she was always in everyone's business. Frances knew she had to work on not meddling so much, or she'd end up like her predecessor who was fired just six months ago for sticking her nose where it shouldn't have been — even after being warned over and over again, and, after signing an agreement upon her hiring ten years ago to keep everything in-house that went on at the Magenta's estate, nicknamed Southwood Hills.

"Yes, Frances, what is it now?" Constance returned, shutting the heavy door and she started to walk beside Frances toward the ten-foot wide, hand-sewn gold-carpeted hallway.

"They're ready for you downstairs. There are a lot of decisions that I believe it would be best for you to make, especially the arrangements in the Great Room. Also, the special tulips from Holland have just arrived. My, you look gorgeous today. Your hair and that yellow sundress fits you to a 'T'."

"Thanks," Constance mumbled mechanically, knowing that she had struggled with her hair, she finally put it in a bun and used her large star shaped diamond earrings, hoping people would notice them instead of her hair.

As they walked down the beige-colored hallway, lined with paintings such as Eugene Galien-Laloue's *La Place du Chatelet*, Frederick Arthur Bridgman's *Les Basses Pyrénées*, and an oil painting by Frans Hals entitled *Gypsy Girl*, all of which were framed in heavy gold and silver.

When they reached the top of the marble staircase, hammers, saws, laughing and yelling could be heard along with the smell of fresh baked bread. They both could see various workmen in uniforms: painters, sign hangers, electricians, movers; all bringing in brown padded folding chairs and workers cleaning windows, light fixtures and furniture, as they made their way down the stairwell which opened to a huge vestibule with twenty-foot ceilings and a chandelier with three layers of lights and mirrors, all polished gold. It was so large it had taken four men to hold it up while it was being installed.

The floor of the vestibule was a tan marble with dark gold veins running through it which ran to two huge white French doors fifteen feet high with stained glass inserts of roses, Constance's favorite flower. The room was supported by four white marble columns with finely carved cornices with cherubs carved in them. In the vestibule were customized designed tables with Italian candelabras of gold and marble, converted into vases.

Constance had marveled that her husband, who spent twenty million dollars building and designing the estate, had told her to spare no expense in decorating the home the way she wanted.

She didn't. She spent a total of five million dollars for the initial designs, antiques, wallpaper, curtains, valences, rugs, chandeliers and general furnishings, but each year she added about one-hundred thousand dollars worth of additional items. Her home was definitely the talk of the town.

When Constance and Frances finally reached the bottom stair, Frances sounded like an excited schoolgirl who had been chosen as head cheerleader. "Isn't this great, Mrs. M!" This is the biggest party I have ever been involved with since I've been here. With the entire RSVP's I've received, the guest list could top 500. It's gonna be great! The rains have ended; the sky is clearing. I'm sure it's going to be a wonderful evening."

"Yes, I'm sure it is," Constantly quietly responded as if she had barely heard Frances, it was as if her mind was somewhere else. "You don't sound very excited. Cheer up Mrs. M. It's gonna be wonderful. What do you think the surprise announcement will be, if you don't mind me asking?" Frances asked, knowing it was alright, but she didn't want to be accused of butting into something that really wasn't her business, but she always tried to make it her business though she did try to be discreet.

"You," Constance said in a business tone of voice, pointing to a young man in a blue and white uniform with white epaulets on his jacket. He was carrying a large vase shaped like a tulip itself. It was full of purple-, yellow- and violet-colored tulips. "Put the one you have in your hand beside the entryway to the dining room and all the bigger ones line up here in the vestibule and the smaller ones in the Great Room there along the baseboard."

"Yes ma'am." The young man smiled with his large ears sticking out from his head full of red hair. He was like most men smitten by Constance's beauty. He lingered a little as if he was waiting for a wink or something. He received nothing but a smile as he watched her turn toward her maid. He went to work.

"Sorry Frances, the announcement, who knows? Charleton could announce anything from a new mall project or a new hotel, some new business venture or who knows, he might want to run for President or Governor."

Without warning, Constance heard shouting over the sound of the saws and hammers coming from the Great Room. Frances and she went there immediately, nearly running into a painter in white overalls stained with blue and red paint wearing a red bandana. "Whoa, Mrs. Magenta, my boys want to know which part of the stage is to be which color," he asked softly.

"Just a minute," Constance said, brushing past him. The yelling was getting louder as she moved toward the Great Room, passing the other two other maids who worked part-time, and they were also dressed just like Frances. They were supposed to be cleaning; instead, they were flirting with two blonde guys hanging the welcome banners and streamers.

"Get to work you two, flirt on your own time!" Constance yelled, pointing at them as she spoke. She entered the Great Room where all the hammering was going on. The sawing was just outside by the breezeway. She saw other workers with tape measures, screw drivers and other instruments of their trade. Many were engaged in building a platform for the conductor of the orchestra and singer and her husband to use for his big announcement. Other workers in white T's and jeans were unrolling wire and putting up speakers for the sound system.

Constance and Frances both saw a small square headed Italian man with no neck, well dressed in an older tux and tails about ready to mix it up with a very large man in a blue jumpsuit with a face as round as a schoolroom clock. He was standing beside a white, full-sized grand piano holding a gold and ivory harp.

"Not there you dufus! Anybody with normal intelligence knows that the harp always goes behind the first violins, not between the second violins and the brass section," the Italian man shouted, pointing his bony and rather crooked finger toward the east wall. He smiled sheepishly under his thick mustache, allowing wrinkles to appear on his mostly bald head with only a wreath of dyed black hair.

"Look Bub, who died and made you king? I already moved your stupid harp three times. Why don't you make up your mind?" the mover returned, becoming frustrated at the indecision.

"Fellas, come on, no need to argue, in case you don't know, I'm Constance Magenta, Charleton's wife," Constance said, standing between them and stretching her arms out trying to keep them apart, realizing that if they got into a fight, the mover would win. He was as thick as an oak tree and the Italian man was about the size of an average sixth grade boy.

"Sorry madam, I'm the new orchestra director at the university, Zen Zeta," he said sheepishly as he continued looking at Constance's overwhelming elegance even though she was dressed modestly. He continued, "I'm in charge of setting up everything for tonight, but this dufus here is making everything difficult; he's as big and dumb as a man can come." Zen Zeta said jeering at the mover, but he squinted for some reason.

"Who are you calling a dufus? All you eggheads, in your case I should say boxhead, you're all just alike, all brains and you still don't know nothin'. You have no concern for the little guy."

"Little guy! I bet you've never been a little guy in your whole life," Zen Zeta shot back, smiling a little but still squinting.

"Now it's fat jokes. You know, I don't need this job bad enough to be insulted by you, you squirt, you modern-day Napoleon. I quit!" The moving man fired back, irritated more than angry. He left the ivory-and-gold-colored harp, and he started to walk out the French doors that led to the back of the estate where his other movers were unloading the orchestra music stands and the larger instruments.

Constance grabbed the mover by his arm and pulled him toward herself as she pleaded, "Don't quit. Come on fellas, at least try to get along. The party is supposed to be a fun event. What is your name?" As she asked questions Zen Zeta started to lash out and hit the big man on his huge arm, squinting as he did so.

The big man really tried to ignore the little man, responding to Constance's questions. "I'm Randy, Randy O'Hanson," Randy said politely, trying to avoid Zen Zeta. Constance's very presence seemed to calm him; she had this effect on people, even though inside she felt quite the opposite. Randy knew he could squash Zen Zeta like a bug, but ignoring him seemed to be the best route, until he intensified his taunting.

"Randy 'O', huh? Maybe the 'O' stands for 'O so fat! Ha! Ha!"

"Enough Mr. Zeta! You love to keep things stirred up, don't you? Do you wear glasses? I noticed you squint a lot. Maybe if you would wear glasses you could really see what's going on. Randy is just here to help you. If you guys settle down, I'll, well, I'll donate to the University Orchestra and Randy, I'll give you a bonus and you and your wife, I noticed your wedding ring, may come tonight and be my guests, agreed?" Constance, smiling timidly, hoping this would resolve the issue.

"Gosh, Patsy will do a back flip being invited to a party like this. Wow! And a bonus too! You're just too kind, Mrs. Magenta. Oh, by the way, how much is the bonus?" Randy asked, almost ready to jump for joy. "Don't worry, I'm very generous."

Zen Zeta glared at both of them and said under his breath, "There goes the neighborhood," then he spoke aloud, "money, money, that's all you muscle heads think about. Fine, with all the university cutbacks, we could use the money. Glasses, I see fine; money big and fat money too."

"Mr. Zeta, I'm warning you, enough is enough. I do know a lot of the curators at the university, I could make it rough on you" Constance said, pointing her finger in his face.

"Okay, okay, can't a guy have any fun? Put the harp right there. We need to leave room for the rest of the strings."

"Whew! I'm glad that's settled," Constance said, sighing in relief. Just then she heard Chef Pierre Edmond, yelling about something from the kitchen. Frances was trying to console him. Constance headed that direction.

Constance arrived in the extra-large modern kitchen, with its large, built-in appliances in black and chrome, a large center island with eight burners and a Viking range, copper bowls and copper bottom pans hanging beneath handmade cabinets along with a full-size upright freezer, a full-size refrigerator, four sinks and dishwashers, and plenty of counter space trimmed in the same black and chrome. Four ovens, now busied by the chef, whose face was constantly frowning, making him look more like Chef Boyardee than Emeril. Even when things were going right, he rarely smiled. He taught at a culinary institute out east but whenever Constance needed the best, she called him.

Chef Pierre occasionally also brought students with him wearing baker's hats and French pastry frocks like him. He was better at deserts, but he could cook anything. One of his students was breaking eggs in a copper bowl. One was retrieving fresh milk from a plastic grocery sack and Chef Pierre was standing near the center island preparing to make Geoduck Sashimi, but first he decided to chop up some mushrooms to make Grilled Minted Lamb Chops and Mushrooms with Pilaf Salad.

"Constance, I can't do it, these mushrooms...sorry to scream at your help. These mushrooms — here, smell this. They're not fresh enough. I've got to have fresh mushrooms."

Constance looked at Chef Pierre, and then she just threw her hands in the air and said, "Oh c'mon, 7:00 o'clock get here soon! Save me, save me!"

After pacifying Chef Pierre by procuring fresher mushrooms by phone, Constance attended to other needs such as seating arrangements for her guests, the placement of the ice sculpture to come and centerpieces. The valets had to be told the parking order, not that they needed to know how to park cars, she just wanted them to do it a certain way.

As mid-afternoon arrived, she was walking through the vestibule headed for the family room which would be used for general overflow, it was one third the size of the Great Room and adorned with mostly family portraits with her two children, from infancy to their current ages, a daughter Teresa, now 32 and her son Teddy, now 28. Constance was interrupted by the door chime, which was so loud it could be heard throughout the entire house. She called to Frances, "I'll get it!"

The door was already opened. She smiled at the blonde headed mail carrier dressed in blue shorts with a yellow stripe going down the side and a blue shirt with his name on it. Constance took the mail and thanked Josh as she looked through it, frowning at bills and advertisements (unless it was something they were already thinking about getting). She began to smile upon seeing a rather fragrant letter, lavender and addressed to her in perfect penmanship. It smelled so nice that she sniffed it twice. Constance looked at the return address and knew exactly who had sent it. She pursed her lips and called for Frances. She immediately entered the vestibule from the family room.

"Yes, Mrs. M?" Frances responded cheerfully.

"Take over; I'll be in the study for a while if you need me. Oh, tell the painters to paint the platform white and gold — that will work, gold around the edges, white on the sides. If you really need me, that is, if there is a real emergency, Frances, I trust you to handle things," Constance said, not acknowledging Frances' response, which was a nod yes, as she walked down the entryway and to the right — trying not to listen to the continuing preparations.

Constance entered her husband's huge study with his walnut bookshelves full of books about building things, from bridges to three level highways. There was a large portrait of her dressed up as an ascot queen, done for charity, over the marble fireplace with black pokers and screens. She glanced at it, as she sat down in her husband's large high-backed button-tufted leather chair, so large she nearly disappeared in it. Matter of fact, if she had her back to the door and someone entered, she couldn't be seen. She noticed how organized his desk was with a PC, flat screen, a large calculator, printer and various chrome structures. One had two figures balancing on a tightrope with a long pole in the first rider's hands. She thought, "if only her life could be so balanced." Constance rolled the chair around on the plastic floor guard and placed the other mail, mostly bills which her husband took care of (he had told her that her only job was to look pretty for him), on the large Maplewood desk. She sighed heavily seeing her husband's ice bucket next to his Glenfiddich Single Malt Scotch Whiskey, which he loved along with Macallan Cask Strength Scotch Whiskey. Her aggravation was caused by the fact that he had never been much of a drinker, but up to and after "the incident" he had begun to drink more, along with another habit which she deemed quite detestable was that he had taken up smoking cigars, evidenced by the wooden glass covered cigar case full of "Davidoff's" the only brand he smoked. She shook her head trying to rid herself of her pet peeves but the sudden image of "the incident" flashed in her mind and made her grow angry for the moment. She looked down at her letter again, the lavender fragrance made her start to smile once more. She picked it up marveling at how near the handwriting was, as if someone had taken extra care making sure the address and name was so perfect as to not offend anyone. Like a grade-schooler turning in a report to a teacher they really liked. As she looked at the return address, she reflected fondly on the memory of the person who had sent the letter. The memory was good, mostly, like the memory of an old friend that had been really close, like a child or a kid sister. There seemed to be a warmth and comfort that rose up inside her. She sank deeper into her husband's chair as if she was being absorbed in a much gentler, kinder world of yesterday. Constance slowly opened the letter, wanting to hurry at first but a flash of a not so positive memory flooded her mind for a moment as if this person had not always been all things good and wonderful. She shook her head, opened the perfectly folded letter, again it was as if the person sending it had taken extra care not to be disrespectful to the recipient. It was as if the sender wanted only the best, the most positive points to come across, that every jot, title, and stamp; everything had been done with thought and not hurried. It was as if this amount of care gave a message itself. Constance began to read:

> Dear Mrs. Magenta,
> I do hope and pray that your family is well? I have been praying much for you lately and I do appreciate you taking the time out of your day to read this letter. There hasn't been a day go by that I hadn't thought about all of you, especially you, because you were always kind and gracious to me when I didn't always respond the same way. Please forgive me for my lack of understanding of my own heart. I will explain myself in the balance of this letter.
> First off, I want to say I have no hard feelings toward anyone, even though (and I'm assuming) that everyone knows how difficult Ted's and my breakup was. I must be totally honest here which I feel is the only way to be. I did love your son very much. He was my first real love. No man had made me feel that way before or since, and if I have offended anyone by the tensions caused by the breakup, I ask your forgiveness. I guess, just being a small-town girl at heart, I just couldn't understand debutante balls, 401K, Roth IRAs and IPOs. At that time, I just didn't get what real love and real life was all about.
> Why we broke up is really not the major issue. The real issue is (and I do regret confessing this since we were not married and it was wrong), I did sleep with your son and I now realize that action brought a lot of heartache to my life, but since that time I have

asked the Lord Jesus Christ to forgive me and to come live in my heart and help me to live differently, and He has. I'm not the same naïve girl I was three years ago. Jesus has truly changed my life and it is for that fact alone I wrote this in an attempt to set the record straight and I don't know how to say this any other way but the night Ted and I slept together I became pregnant and you now have a 2 year old grandson named Theodore Lee Magenta, Jr. and he looks just like his father. I know this is all probably a lot to comprehend right now but I felt compelled to let you know. My father has said that I really needed to try and make contact again with your family because you have the right to a relationship with Pookie, that's what I call him.

I tried so hard to let Ted know but when I first told him I was pregnant I thought he would be happy, but he wasn't. He went ballistic. I had never seen him so angry. He said some really horrible things, he even told me to abort the child, his child. I just couldn't do it, and I continued life as usual because I believe every life is sacred and only the 'Giver of Life' can take it.

Pookie is so cute. I wouldn't trade him for anything in the world. It has taken me a long time to work through that horrible night, but I have, and with God's help and my dad's, I'm moving forward with my life.

I really tried to tell Ted, but he refused my phone calls, he returned letters unopened, and the last straw was when I couldn't even get past his front gate. I gave up. I thought I'd be better off raising Pookie as a single parent. However, I feel differently now. Maybe the time is right to reach out again. My heart is at peace, and I understand it better, and I thought starting with you would be best because, in spite of my many phone calls, you were never rude, you were always gracious, and you never intentionally pushed me away. I thank you for that.

If you agree, I would like to meet with you to see where our relationship will go from here. As far as I know, Ted is unaware of any of this, but every child needs a father. It has been said that some friends last for a while, but only true friends last for eternity and beyond. I would like our friendship to one day be like that.

Please call me at your convenience. Again, I appreciate your time because I feel you have the right to know and to love Pookie as I do.

Respectfully yours,

Tonya Green

P.S. My phone number is 573 555 0199

Constance put the letter down unsure of the gravity of it all, having liked Tonya. But at times her lack of maturity caused her some discomfort, but the worst part was that her own son had said nothing about this entire episode. Emotionally she felt like she had just been run over by a Mack truck. To think she now had a grandson of which she had missed his first steps, his first birthday and his first tooth, and what about all the Christmas presents she could have bought him. To be left out of the actual delivery process. She had been in on all of her daughter's deliveries.

Constance felt a part of her life had been cut out, like a person with selective amnesia, all encased in the thought her relationship with her son, whom she had considered close, now distanced as if they had started on a trek to the North Pole but ended up at the South Pole instead. She felt Tonya was telling the truth because, unfortunately, Teddy did have a temper like his father. Sometimes his face would tighten, and his eyes would get red if he didn't get his way. "What about Charleton?" she thought to herself as she slowly stood up and folded the letter, and then she began to shake as she talked to herself. "Oh, if Charleton finds out it's not going to be good. He told me what he'd do to me if he ever found out that one of our children had a child out of wedlock and he does make good on his threats. How in the world can I keep this from him and Teddy? They both will have to be told eventually. I'll be hated as surely as the world, by both of them. Why Lord? Why do these things always happen to me?"

Constance started to cry, just as she heard a knock on the door and the soft but hurried voice of Frances say, "Sorry to disturb you Mrs. M, but Chef Pierre wants better Geoduck clams for his Geoduck Sashimi and the two men are arguing again at the orchestra platform."

Constance sighed, wiped her face and tried to pull herself together. She picked her letter up and slid it into a safe place under the top of her sundress, as if she wanted no one else to be aware of the letter's existence. Then she responded through the heavy door to Frances, "Yes, I'll be right there, geez." Still trying to regain her composure because of this emotional earthquake she mumbled to herself as she started to open the door. "When O' Lord is my life ever going to be worry-free? When Lord?"

Chapter 4

"What! How can you lose a bulldozer and a scraper and what, rebar is missing too — gee — find it! Find them! Who in the world could be stealing from me... How?

What? That's what I pay you for — now find out what's going on — geez." Charleton said, slamming the phone down as his chest heaved in disbelief. He walked around his spacious office at his corporate headquarters at Highway 763 on the south side of Columbia, Missouri.

Charleton Magenta looked out of the large gold-tinted windows to see the busy grounds - full of metal, brick and steel buildings, full of trucks, cars and grounds keepers all in gold uniforms with large black 'M's on their sleeves. He smiled briefly at his accomplishments — gazing on, he admired the fine sculptured hedges that framed the long concrete driveway which ran in a circle around a three-tiered fountain with a large statue of Atlas holding up the world and arching across the top of the world. Arching across the world was a sign "Magenta Inc. — Building A Better Way". Beyond that, Charleton saw the employee parking lot that held a thousand cars, mostly new. He smiled; he knew it was because he paid his employees the highest salaries in the industry.

He had 5 other offices: Quincy Illinois, Des Moines Iowa, Jefferson City, Moberly and Springfield Missouri. His employees seem to appreciate this constant growth; many had been with him for over twenty years.

He knew it wasn't all due to his own intellect. He had decided to expand into bigger projects. He had consulted his father who had been a heavy bridge engineer for years. Both felt it was appropriate to branch out into other avenues of construction.

Charleton knew he had been blessed with a mind that had to be stimulated quite often. This was the reason he remembered all of his heavy equipment. He also had a quick wit that seemed to get him into or out of trouble, whichever he chose to use it for. Above all he hated to fail at anything; he was a sore loser. His father had told him, when he was just starting sandlot ball, "think like a loser and you'll be a loser". This was something he conveyed to everyone that he worked or did business with.

Charleton turned his gaze back to the room, rolling his eyes concerning his just ended conversation. He stared at his red oriental rugs, large, overstuffed chairs and his paintings of the great ships of the 1700s trying to think of something else, but he really couldn't. He stopped at a long wooden framed mirror, admiring his six-foot-five-inch frame, carrying two hundred-and-seventy pounds, twenty more than he felt necessary to be considered svelte.

Charleton had peppered black hair. He had tried to fight the grey but finally gave up. He wore a thin penciled mustache with a little wisp of hair under his bottom lip. His sideburns were long and at an angle, if anyone asked about his sideburns, he would say it was his tribute to Elvis, his favorite singer.

Charleton put his hands in the pockets of his French designer suit. He said he didn't like the American designers, except Bill Blass, the rest just weren't daring enough.

The intercom buzzed and he quit admiring himself. He began to think about the thief and more. He walked over to the intercom. "Yes Ellie, what is it now? Another headache?"

"No sir. A Mrs., sorry, a Miss Rose LaVon is here to see you."

"Rose LaVon, boy that's sure a pretty name. I hope she's as pretty as she sounds!" Charleton said suddenly, primping up a bit, running his fingers through his hair and checking his breath into his hands. He then adjusted his tailored tie and continued, "Who is she?"

"She's a reporter with what newspaper, ma'am?" She turned to ask Miss LaVon, "She's a reporter for the World Press."

"O' fine," Charleton responded weakly as if his balloon had burst. "A member of the press, she probably wants to meddle in my affairs again." He muttered to himself.

Just then, the main door to his office opened. A tall gorgeous impeccably dressed young woman in a grey business suit trimmed in white, knocked softly, then stepped in. Her hair was cut short, just below the ears. Each ear ringed with five white star earrings. She wore a smidge of makeup and just a kiss of lipstick. Her eyes were very large and round, with long eyelashes.

"Hello Mr. Magenta, I'm Rose LaVon," she said smiling, showing her perfectly straight white teeth.

"Yeah — that's right — uh — have a seat," Charleton said, smitten by her beauty. When he passed her chair, her fragrance enamored him. He then continued, "What brings you to my office Mrs. LaVon?"

"It's Miss, I'm not married nor have any plans to in the near future. You can call me Rose. Everyone can remember a Rose."

"Yes, Rose. A rose by any other name would smell so ..." Charleton mumbled the last part to himself acting like a giddy schoolboy, hoping she didn't hear him. He cleared his throat and continued, "You can call me Charleton if you like. Pardon my manners! Would you like something to drink?"

Charleton watched her shake her head no. He then proceeded to fix himself one from a silver and gold tray on his desk. The ice was in a silver sculptured bucket. He put some ice in a gold glass and poured something from a smoke-colored pitcher with a glass handle into his gold glass.

"Iced tea, best drink in the world, I'm trying to get off the hard stuff. I only drink the hard stuff when I'm really, really stressed out and I'm starting to get there today with everything going on. Now little 'lady' I mean Rose, what do you need to see me about? Please, have a seat." Charleton watched her closely as she sat down. He went to the chair behind her and nearly stumbled over himself getting there, as men seem to do when they meet an irresistible woman.

"I appreciate you seeing me on such short notice. My newspaper would like to do a feature story on you. Your rag to riches story is incredible. In less than thirty years your company is worth ten billion dollars. Your employee turnover is less than two percent. That is incredible!" Rose said, obviously impressed as she now sat across from Charleton who seemed a bit nervous.

"Yes. Some days I can't believe it either. But I believe God helps those who help themselves." Charleton said watching her shift her weight in the brown overstuffed chair in the front of the desk.

"Are you a religious man?" Rose asked.

"No, I just believe the man upstairs watches out for those with a pure heart," Charleton said, trying hard not to stare at her gorgeous figure. "Excuse me Rose, I know this isn't politically correct but, you're the most beautiful woman I've ever seen. I hope I haven't offended you."

"No, none taken, God made me this way. So, I thank Him for the way I look." Rose said rather stoically, seemingly not offended by his rather personal remarks."

"That's a good answer. When did you want to do this story? Today is not a good day. I've got a problem at the Carrington Lane site north of Canton, Missouri." Before Charleton could finish, the phone rang. He excused himself and answered, speaking roughly, "What! How can that be, a bulldozer! Another bulldozer! What! They don't just get up and walk off! Look Carl, keep checking around. Geez. I'd better make a quick trip up there. Look, you handle things until I get there," Charleton said, growing quite irritated by this continuing problem. He looked at Rose who had an inquisitive look on her face.

"Is everything alright?" she asked softly.

"No, it isn't! Look, I need to cut this interview short. I've got a situation I need to go take care of. It'll take about 3 hours round trip to take care of it. Some other time, okay?"

"Look, wait, I'm having a big bash at my estate, a formal affair. Take one of my business cards. I'll write down my address, stop by then. We should be able to talk. It's at 7:00pm. Just go south about 5 miles past the M.U. Stadium. We're on the left, the big house with the stone wall and the rod iron gate with the big 'M' on it". Charleton said, taking his business card from a small glass holder on his desk, shaped like a whale and writing down all he had just told her.

"I heard it through the grapevine that you have a big announcement to make. Some are saying you're going to throw your hat in the ring." Rose said, getting up as he watched. Charleton got up and moved towards the door.

"How do you people find out so much? Look, just come by and we'll talk." Charleton said, shaking his head as he opened the door to enter the hallway where Ellie was waiting with her large glasses on the end of her nose. She always wore them that way when she looked at people.

"Elle, call Joe. Tell him to bring the car around front. I need to go out to the Carrington Lane site. Cancel all my other appointments. Goodbye Rose. We'll talk later." Charleton said, looking at her briefly then heading for the door, leaving her behind as if she wasn't even there.

Chapter 5

The Carrington Lane project 115 miles north of Columbia was huge. It was a highway development that would connect Canton, Missouri with a four-lane road coming out of Iowa eventually. This particular site seemed to be hit with a lot of thefts lately.

Charleton's white limo with gold trimmed wheels pulled up to the foreman's trailer with a few company pickups alongside the trailer — some old, some new. There was a sign declaring all the hazardous materials on site and all the business permits required and three portable toilets.

Behind the trailers, the graders, the bulldozers and other earth moving equipment were very busy pushing dirt and tossing dust into the air. Even though it had rained in town they didn't get any at that location.

Carl the foreman met Charleton at the door. His skin was hard and red from all the years he'd spent in the sun. His face was grizzled with heavy lines around his eyes which of late, looked tired and bloodshot. For sixty-four he was still quite spry. He welcomed Charleton into the trailer full of blueprints, maps, an old coffee maker, old tables and chairs sitting on a muddy floor with a telephone on the small desk near the two windows which were open wide.

"Carl — what's going on? Have you found out anything new since we last talked?" Charleton asked, watching Carl move his hard hat off his sun-bleached hair. He then pulled out a soaked handkerchief and wiped his face off.

"I don't get it boss, lately it seems like everyday something comes up missing. I know you can't put a bulldozer in your back pocket. I just don't get it." Carl said, shaking his head in disbelief.

"Carl, we can't just keep absorbing these losses and it's not just here, it's our road-widening project on Nifong Boulevard. It's the same thing. We lost all the rebar and one water wagon, and now this. Did anyone see anything?" Charleton asked, looking out the windows to see a new kid on the road-grader dressed in the traditional navy-blue pants and shirt for the road construction division with Magenta, Inc. above the right pocket and the person's name above the left pocket.

"Who's the new guy on the grader?"

Carl turned and looked also, then said, "That's Danner — Danner Colter, a great kid. He loves to put in overtime. He's not new, he's been around for a year now. He reminds me of myself when I was younger," Carl said, watching him move the levers back and forth with ease.

"That's good — but we've really got to stop these thefts. They hurt everybody and I don't have time to come up here every day. I guess we're gonna have to bring in our own security. The sheriff and his deputies aren't making the rounds enough. Carl, I really can't do much here but let me know if anything more suspicious happens. I really want to ring the necks of the people or persons doing this! You don't take from Charleton Magenta and get away with it. See you, Carl."

"Yeah, boss, I'll keep my eyes peeled," Carl said — but for some reason that last comment bothered him.

"Carl, one more thing: Are you all right? If I may say so, you don't look so good. You look pretty tired. I'm sorry about your messy divorce — pretty ugly huh." Charleton said, placing his large hand on Carl's shoulder.

"Yeah, I guess it hurts worse when it's totally unexpected. You know what I got for my 40th wedding anniversary?"

"What?" Charleton asked honestly not knowing the answer.

"My divorce papers tied around a champagne bottle. Forty years down the drain. I thought she loved me. We never fought. I always came home. Sure, I drank a little now and then. I really thought she was happy. Then, POW! All she said is 'I don't love you anymore and I never did.' Hit me like a freight train," Carl said sadly, seeing the brokenness of the moment before him.

"Take heart, if I can do anything for you let me know." Charleton said, patting Carl on the back while he exited the trailer.

"Thanks Boss, I will." Carl said softly realizing that his boss really meant it. He smiled briefly then went back to work, forgetting his previous concern.

Chapter 6

As soon as Charleton got back in his limo, still wondering who and why someone would steal from his company, he received a phone call from the General who wanted to see him at his home today. He agreed though time was slipping away.

As he put his cell phone in his coat pocket, he couldn't help but smile about the General whose real name was Dudley Vincent. He received the name General because he loved to play army and pretend he was president as a kid. However, when he was drafted to serve in WWII, his weak kidneys kept him out. But he still loved politics.

The General never did run for any office because he said he was too skinny, to ugly and lacked a formal education. Only the ugly and skinny may have been true by some because he had a large forehead, no hair and a W.C. Fields nose. He was 5 feet 5 inches and 100 pounds. When it came to politics it was said nothing from Boone County to Cole County moved without his knowledge. At seventy-four years of age, he was still very active in the political world.

He was mostly a Democrat since the Days of Truman. In the 80's he loved Ronald Reagan and not only did he like domestic politics, but he also dabbled in foreign affairs.

It had been his father that headed the delegation to bring Winston Churchill to deliver his famous "Iron Curtain" speech in Fulton, Missouri in 1946, defending the barrier thrown up by the USSR around the nations of Eastern Europe. His father had taken him over to meet Winston Churchill, a round-faced man who was wearing a hat with a black rim at the base and was smoking a fat cigar. His father had met him once at his home at Chartwell, he being a foreign correspondent. He told Winston that his son wanted to be just like him. Winston smiled and nodded his head, "That's fine." And he shook the young man's hand.

The young man, now the General, liked the firm grip and stoic nature of Churchill so much that he wanted to be just like him. He really loved Churchill, especially for his no-backing-down policy with Hitler. However, he despised Neville Chamberlain, whose appeasement of Hitler led to the Munich Pact.

The General was getting up in years and his health wasn't the best, but he wanted one last try at getting things right in Jefferson City. He had watched the news of Charleton's success, and he heard some were hinting he should run for political office. He really liked his ambition, and he felt he could help him achieve that. They had spoken for hours and became good friends, meeting at a fundraiser for Ronald Reagan's first presidential try in the late 70's. He called him Charlie because he kind of thought of him as a son more than anything. He felt Charlie had lots of potential. He was noble, honorable and true.

Charleton pulled up through the rustic gates of the old estate of pink and white, looking like cotton candy. It was in need of a little paint. It reminded one of an old antebellum estate in the Deep South. He saw the General sitting on his porch in a rocking chair with a plaid shawl across his lap. He seemed to always be cold; and wore a knit cap on his bald head all the time, which he always said it was to keep his brains warm. His distractors said, however, it was to keep his brains from falling out. He wore glasses of late, and recently he started using a walker to get around.

"Hello General," Charleton said, as he walked up the crumbling steps of the estate and smiled at the lonely but cheerful man. He reached out to shake his hand.

"Hey Charlie, come on up. Have a seat. Mable, bring our guest some tea." The General said, talking through the front door screen and seeing no one. He turned back to Charleton and reached his frail arm covered in a light blue shirt, barely getting above a small white round table with two metal chairs to shake Charleton's hand.

"Sure is a nice day, huh, General?" Charleton said, sitting next to him, nodding to the hunchbacked caretaker who smiled briefly, dressed darkly, bringing out tea.

"Yes Charlie, I do appreciate you coming to see me. Old people like me get forgotten, you know."

"There's no way I'd ever forget you. You've been a good friend for over twenty years now. You've been like a father to me," Charleton said truthfully as he sipped some tea from a glass trimmed in white. He never added sugar though the caretaker brought more out.

"Well son, are you ready for tonight?" This truly could be the start of something big. Who knows?" One day you might live at 1600 Pennsylvania Avenue," the General grinned showing all his false teeth.

"Could be? Someday! My wife's getting everything ready for tonight. Everybody who's anybody is going to be there. I hope you are coming!" Charleton asked, really hoping he would.

"Seven o'clock is a little past my bedtime. Parties are for the young. Hey, I heard Phyllis DeJayne is going to sing. I saw her years ago in a touring company of "Seven Brides for Seven Brothers." They stopped in St. Louis when I lived there. My, was she a fair creature and could she sing! I even got to talk to her backstage since my father was a member of the press. He didn't always cover politics you know," the General said fondly reflecting on his memory of her. He leaned back looking at his willow trees in his front yard.

"No, this isn't her that's singing. This is her granddaughter, Phyllis. She's every bit as beautiful. This Phyllis DeJayne is only 21 years old. She attends the University. My wife saw her at a fundraiser for the General Scholarship Fund last month where she was the featured singer. She just had to have her come and sing for us. I'm sure you didn't ask me over here to discuss heart throbs."

"Yeah, you're right. I hate to bring this up, but the rumors are flying that one of the 'rag' papers is out to get some dirt on you. Don't ask me why. It seems like when a person is successful the bullets start flying, someone always wants to gun the big shots down. Funny, years ago people liked good stories, but now it seems like some Americans just can't wait to read trash. It seems Americans can't rejoice when others have good fortune. I'm not sure who she is or what newspaper or magazine she works for but just be alert. As I've told you many times, I might be a lot of things, but I'll never be known as a crooked politician. I believe in our government, and I believe in our state motto: 'Salus Populi Suprema Lex Esto.' I'm sure my Latin's rusty, but it means 'Let the welfare of the people shall be the Supreme Law.'"

"I believe with my whole heart, scandal, any scandal, tramples and scars those who want to do right whether it's the Teapot Dome or the Monica scandal. Both damage pure politics."

"I just want you to make sure you keep your nose clean, that there are no skeletons in your closet and that your family is 100% behind you on this."

"The year is 2003; people want honesty and integrity, not a bunch of hot air. How do your wife and kids feel about all this? They are behind you one hundred percent, aren't they?" the General asked, looking Charleton in the eye.

Charleton paused and got up and stretched as if this question made him uncomfortable. "No problem, they know me, and they know I will always do the right thing."

The General accepted his answer knowing Charleton himself. The General spoke again, "Excellent! Look, let me know how the party goes. I've got my boys snooping around a bit to find out who this 'plant' is that's trying to hurt your chances. I wouldn't put Barney past doing something like this. He's hated me ever since I voted for old Ronald. When is ever going to learn it's not the party, it's the candidate that counts? Anyway son, just be yourself and live like the good Lord above is watching every moment of your life, because he is."

~

As Constance sat in front of her lighted vanity preparing for the party, she was putting a little highlight around her cheeks that complimented her golden skin tone. She had plucked her eyebrows. Then with an eyebrow pencil, she made them thinner as she left the center just above her cute nose. She added eyeliner and a little eye shadow to make her brown eyes rounder and seductive. She had twirled her hair around the top of her head to make her most elegant with only two curls dangling in front of her small ears which had two large diamonds, one in each ear. They were trimmed in 14-carat gold shaped like half-moons; all tied together with just a kiss of extra silky lipstick.

Her dress was solid black, hanging to the edge of her shoulders showing her bare arms. It was long and flowing, showing her shapely figure quite well. It was Paris original, framed by a handcrafted, mostly square, gold necklace from Florence, Italy with diamonds along the edge and in the center. Her shoes were black with jeweled trim and highlights.

She reached over and sprayed her Vanderbilt perfume. She stood and walked over to the full-length closet mirror. She smiled, knowing how gorgeous she really was. She remarked to herself, "I could give a twenty-five-year-old a run for her money."

Constance laughed a little out loud knowing that through the course of the day she had gotten in a better mood. Around 5:00 pm everything was set, only the items that needed to be refrigerated were not yet on the long buffet tables in the dining room, so she had come upstairs to get ready.

It was now 6:15 pm, and her husband was still in the shower, she thought, but with her mugging in the mirror she had not realized that he had gotten out of the shower and had put on his tuxedo pants and ruffled shirt and had snuck behind her smiling. Her mind, as it often did, floated back and forth from feeling great about herself to feeling lousy. "Oh hon, you startled me. I didn't even hear you get out of the shower and get dressed."

"No problem. Are you the most gorgeous woman tonight or what? You'll definitely be the 'Belle' of the ball." Charleton said, twirling his wife around to look her over.

"Thanks. You want your tie straightened?" Constance asked, smiling back as he nodded yes. He did look good, freshly shaven and perky.

"What's the big announcement anyway?" Constance asked, continuing to tie his round ascot tie, quite colorful.

"No, uh, uh, you'll just have to wait like the rest. Don't worry. Put it this way, our whole lives will change for the better. That's all I'll say for now, thanks Babe, you did good," Charleton said, turning away from his wife to put on his tuxedo jacket that was lying across the bed in a plastic bag. He undid the bag and started to put his jacket on.

"Lives changed," Constance mumbled to herself as a thousand scenarios danced through her head — mostly all bad — from her husband leaving her for a new building project in Costa Rica, to a new mall project in Nova Scotia. She mumbled louder, this time so her husband could hear. "Lives changed! What changes? You know I don't like changes!"

"Changes — aww this will be a good change for you and me." Charleton said in a soft tone seeing his wife grow disturbed, confused and angry.

She blurted back, "how do you even know what's best for me? You hardly even talk to me anymore, unless it's just before bedtime." Constance paused for a moment watching her husband adjust his jacket looking into the triple dresser mirror. She saw him put his silk handkerchief in the right pocket of his jacket and another in the right rear pocket of his trousers along with his gold monogrammed money clip with $2000 worth of $100 bills (which he always carried) both of which he had gotten from the first drawer of the cherry wood triple dresser.

He turned towards her and said, "Don't even start. This is no time for an argument. Can't we just enjoy ourselves at least once without being at each other's throat? Let's at least pretend we're a happy couple." Charleton said then he turned away from her and headed toward the door.

"Pretend, pretend! Am I supposed to pretend that I'm happy when I'm with you? Am I supposed to pretend that I'm a Barbie Doll with a fake smile and everything is right with the world? Who are you kidding?" Constance blurted back, growing angrier as she watched her husband start to open the door.

"C'mon, don't even go there. If that's the case, why don't you pretend I bought you that Citation 650 Jet so you could fly around the country to purchase a bunch of old junk that just clutters up the house anyway, and what about that Maserati Spyder that I just bought you for your last birthday? Are you going to pretend I bought you that too? Or are you going to pretend I tried to get Wolfgang Puck and Emeril Lagasse out here just to make dinner for your women's group but all the money in the world can't woo some people. I have given you everything and now the biggest night of my life has come, and you want to argue with me."

"I get so sick and tired of us arguing. I've tried to make you happy over the years. I've come to the inescapable conclusion; how much is my responsibility to make you happy and how much is your own!" Charleton said, looking at his wife whose face was flushed with anger as she stared back into his face.

"What do you know about making me happy? You just think I'm so stupid! My happiness? You sure didn't think of my happiness when you slept with that, that, I'm too much of a lady to use the right word for her, that you-know-what in Memphis. Did you really think I was that dense, that I when I unpacked your clothes and found a bottle of Chloe' perfume, which I never use, and matter of fact I never liked, along with red frosty lip gloss which I found on your French cut white shirt. Did you really think I would overlook them? What kind of woman do you think I am?" Constance asked, watching her husband carefully. He shook his head, rolled his eyes and then said, "That's low. That was over five years ago. I had too much to drink. I made a mistake and…" Constance jumped in, "a mistake — that's not a mistake! A mistake is putting on the wrong color socks or taking a wrong turn in your car. You deliberately slept with her. Five or fifty years ago, it doesn't matter, a woman just doesn't forget! How could you even think about kissing me and then making love to me after you've been with that strange woman? Why, she could have given you AIDS and then you'd pass it on to me!"

"Alright. Alright. How long do I have to be punished for my sin? Babe, I love you! I really do! Let's just calm down, we've got a party to go to," Charleton said to defuse the tense situation.

"Alright. Things are not all right between us and I'm beginning to think they never will be. You just don't get it, do you! The only thing I ever wanted was you! Not planes, cars, tennis courts or yachts!"

"When you slept with her you rejected me. You stomped on my heart. A woman's heart is fragile like a rose, and you trampled it. I just can't get over it — okay. Part of me wants to reach out and still love you and part of me wants to walk away from you. Sometimes even run away from you forever." Constance said, reflective as she started to cry.

"Now, now don't cry. We'll talk about this later." Charleton said slowly walking over to his wife, while removing his handkerchief from his pocket. He began to wipe some tears away from her eyes which were just starting to make her mascara run. He dampened his kerchief with his tongue in an effort to save her makeup. "Stop crying, your face is going to look like a watercolor painting. I need my Babe to be the 'Belle' of the ball. Remember, you've got to be perfect tonight. I'm counting on you. You are the wife of Charleton Magenta." Charleton said in a rather grandiose tone.

After wiping his wife's face, he then embraced her and kissed her tenderly on the left cheek, she melted into his big arms.

"Oh Charleton, hold me. Hold me forever. I don't know why I say the things I do sometimes. I really do love you." Constance said embracing her husband tightly heaving and feeling his sincerity.

"Everything will be fine Babe. C'mon, we really need to go downstairs and show the whole world how the Magentas' throw a party." Charleton said breaking loose from his wife. He looked at her and smiled briefly as he reached for her hand. They exited the room, at least for the moment pretending to be happy.

As Constance and Charleton descended the staircase, all the guests in the vestibule noticed how beautiful the couple looked. It was as if they had just stepped off a five-tiered wedding cake.

The stairwell was wide enough for four people. The banisters were trimmed in gold and silver that seemed to shimmer in the light of the large chandelier. The gentlemen were in tux and tails, the ladies wore black and white flowing dresses garnished with diamonds, pearls and gold. They made the marble vestibule sparkle. Every few minutes the huge French doors would open up to the front of the estate to greet more guests, who were having their Lincoln's, Cadillac's and Mercedes parked by the valet men dressed in red vests with white shirts and black bow ties.

Maids and servers weaved through the crowd expertly offering a wide variety of drinks in various shaped glasses on gold and silver trays.

Tulips decorated the vestibule leading into the Great Room, where the main party was, they were radiant and smelled wonderful like a walk in the meadow.

As they reached the vestibule, they were greeted by smiles and hugs from friends old and new. Both Charleton and Constance were gracious to everyone.

Before they could get across the hall, they were stopped by Doc Ellis. He was a short stocky man whose pants were always too long, so they dragged the ground causing him to walk on the back of them, which made them fray.

Also, he had a rather annoying habit of saying "don't cha know" after every sentence, which had caused him to lose friends over the years.

Constance and Charleton were just greeted by him.

"Oh Constance you are so beautiful don't cha know." Doc Ellis said while admiring her head to toe.

"Why thank you, I'm glad you could come, where is your better half?" asked Constance, turning and seeing a tall, rotund woman in a black dress with sequins, white pearls and earrings. She had just come from the bathroom in the vestibule.

"Here I am. Is hubby bothering you? Oh, you two look stunning. Wherever did you get that dress?" Mrs. Ellis asked, smiling as she leaned over and hugged Constance.

"It's an original design of a protégé of Lloyd Klein of Paris; you look great yourself," Constance returned honestly.

"Yes — my Gert always looks good — don't cha know." Doc Ellis said, still eyeing Constance he continued. "Charleton you'd better keep your eye on her tonight — don't cha know. Somebody might just swoop down through the window in the party room and take her home, don't cha know."

"Oh shush hubby. I'll be the only one doing the swooping. Let's let them enjoy the rest of the party and put your eyes back in your head — you've got me at home." Gert said, grabbing Doc and leading him as they walked away. Doc Ellis rolled his eyes making sure his wife didn't see him. However, before he got too far away, he leaned over and kissed Constance's hand and waved at her as he and his wife went toward the Great Room.

"Enjoy the party you two." Constance said, as she and her husband, still side by side, moved towards the Great Room, which was flowing with bodies. The orchestra was playing music from Tchaikovsky's 'Swan Lake'.

"Babe, excuse me, there's ol' Walking Joe Teasdale over by the fireplace. Who could mistake his broad shoulders? I'd like to talk to him a bit," Charleton said, leaning over to his wife and brushing her cheek with a kiss.

"Fine" Constance said softly — then mumbled, "There he goes, leaving me alone again." Then she ran into Randy the harp mover and his wife, who were elegantly dressed, him in a black tuxedo that was a hair tight. Her in an evening gown, antiquated with pearls — which seemed a little gaudy — but with the light of her smile (missing a tooth) shown brightly.

"Oh, Patsy, this is Mrs. Magenta. We have her to thank," Randy said as he took a drink from a passing tray.

"Thank you, ma'am, I never dreamed I'd ever come to a shindig like this! My, you're prettier than a lightning bug at midnight. Your house is like one I see on those shows about the rich and famous. This is truly a night to remember," Patsy said, bending down as if kneeling before royalty.

"Oh, that's not necessary, I'm glad you came. Randy and Patsy, I believe it was, enjoy yourselves. I like your pearls. If you need anything just ask, sorry to rush off — lots of guests to greet. Just make yourselves at home."

Constance shook her head, trying to enjoy herself as she entered the Great Room hugging and smiling at everyone she met. As Constance moved gracefully through the crowd, she noticed that many cliques had already formed. Especially a group of mostly heavy bearded old men with bellies that shook when they talked, they had gathered under a painting by Casper Friedrich entitled, "Man and Woman Gazing at the Moon." They all laughed and some roared at some sort of joke — a one-eyed man — with no hair told about the latest dilemma of the current administration in Washington.

Constance watched some women stare at the highly polished instruments in the orchestra; the chandeliered light seemed to reflect off both the woodwinds and brass.

The conductor was a tall white-haired gentleman with a full white mustache. He was one of the founders of MossPac — a symphony group at the University. The way he seemed so animated — everyone knew he was conducting. Constance smiled and tried to be gracious — shaking hands and hugging more people — some she didn't even know personally. However, since this was the upper crust of society she should get to know them, being one of "them" now.

The women also formed cliques. Constance overheard them discuss the latest fashions and the odd color of hair — one woman remarked, "I believe some girls must use Easter egg dye."

Constance chuckled at this, realizing it was probably true with all the bright colors of hair she'd seen lately. As she looked around, all the guests seemed to be having a great time. The ribbons of Red, White and Blue hung from the ceiling. Flowers of every color and shape sat on every windowsill and flat surface in the room. Every vase was a different color.

Constance glanced in the dining room to see long tables covered in blue and white tablecloths with tassels on the end. She could see rows and rows of foods on the snack table which looked so good. She walked over to the doorway to see silver trays full of bruschetta, beef with walnuts topped with kiwi and crab stuffed mushrooms. There was clam dip, seafood dip, and hot broccoli soup served with a variety of chips, crackers, pretzels and fresh breads. The table was so long her eyes seemed to flow naturally to all the main dishes on silver and gold trays. One was a Peach Glazed Virginia Ham. There was Rack of Lamb with Dijon-Mustard Sauce, a bowl full of hot and spicy Arroz Con Pollo and so many other foods wonderfully cooked and garnished. Only the dessert table surpassed them for pure elegance.

There was chocolate ganache, triple layer fudge, Godiva Truffles and much more displayed with passion by Master Chef

Pierre Edmond — who saw Constance standing in the doorway as he roamed the table making sure everything was fine. He gave her the okay sign — then mouthed "I finally got my fresh mushrooms, thanks."

Constance gave him the okay sign back as she smiled at him. She stood there looking at the drink table with its cappuccino, foreign coffees and teas which were in the center of a large ice sculpture of a swan. All the vessels were gold and silver. Everything looked magnificent. The servers were all dressed in white shirts and black pants. Constance noticed how happy the guests were to be served on the finest china along with golden silverware as she watched them eat then smile, she knew they were enjoying themselves.

Constance walked back into the Great Room looking for her husband who was still talking to former Governor Joe Teasdale — she waved to him — both her husband and the former Governor waved back, but it was only her husband who frowned as if she had just interrupted the first NATO conference.

Constance mumbled to herself — "there he goes again, ignoring me."

She heard the music change to Sergei Prokofiev's "Love for three Oranges." As she entered, she immediately noticed Zen Zeta, the awful short man that had been a nuisance earlier that day. She hadn't seen him in her first pass through the Great Room. She noticed how he was flirting with Miss Phyllis DeJayne, who had just entered, looking resplendent in a white gown with beads all over it. She was wearing diamonds trimmed in pearl, and her hair was braided on the top of her head.

Constance noticed that she looked quite older than twenty-one, a fact Zen Zeta had obviously missed being that he should have known it for a very good reason.

"Hi Mr. Zeta, remember me?" Constance said, teasing a bit as Zen Zeta was talking gibberish trying to impress Miss DeJayne. He ignored her for the moment. "Oh — sorry Mrs. Magenta — I didn't see you coming. Isn't she gorgeous? I would really like to marry her — but she gives me no attention." Zen Zeta said, trying to grab her hand with gold fingernails. Miss DeJayne slapped him away.

"Stop, I'm not interested, don't you recognize me? I'm in your music theory class, Tuesday afternoons." Miss DeJayne said growing tired of his pestering.

"You are? My glasses, where are my glasses? Zen Zeta asked, searching through his black tuxedo until he found them. He put them on and then looked at her again, and said, "Oh, Phyllis I'm so sorry, I'm an old man sometimes my mind goes. I won't bother you again."

"Sure," Phyllis said smiling as he finally left her, she continued "what an irritating little man. Mrs. Magenta, I've never been to a bash like this, wow!" Phyllis said, as she looked around, seeing the Curators wife, the Dean of Students, heads of departments and their wives, and some of her professors jokingly seemingly for the first time.

"Yes, you look so pretty. I bet your grandmother is so proud of you."

"Yes, she is. You know she was so sorry that mother wasn't interested in singing, but she sure is glad I picked it up. I love it! I try to remember what Grandma always says," Phyllis said, stopping to purse her lips, to make her look like her famous grandmother, "honey, God gives you a talent — if you don't use it — you'll lose it."

They both chuckled as did a few onlookers. "What are you going to sing tonight?" Constance asked, watching the orchestra play skillfully.

"Well, that's a surprise. It'll be something you like I'm sure, oh — excuse me Mrs. Magenta — I'll be singing in a few minutes; I need to warm up," Phyllis said, hugging her warmly as women do who honestly like each other.

Constance finally decided to get a drink as her maid, Frances, went by with a full tray, "Great party, huh, Mrs. M?"

"Yes Frances, you guys did great. Everything's going great so far," before Constance could finish talking she turned around to see a woman she had never seen — tall and gorgeous with blonde hair that was perfectly styled, and she had a soft white sheer dress on that fit her just right, as if it had been designed just for her; it was slightly off white and it had flowers from the knee down, which showed her well-tanned skin. She wore gold earrings and very little makeup. She was the type of woman everyone in the room knew was naturally beautiful. Before Constance could introduce herself, her husband seemingly came out of nowhere to make the formal introduction.

'Babe, this is Rose LaVon. She's a reporter with — who — oh — the World Press; she wants a story on me — on us," Charleton said, smiling sheepishly for some reason.

"Hi Mrs. Rose, may I?" Constance said graciously, she continued "that's a great name you have."

"Yes, you may, and it's Miss. I met your husband at the office, but he was too busy to talk to me there today, so he invited me here tonight to talk to him about his life. My, you have a lovely home. God truly has blessed you," Rose said looking around the Great Room to see the fine paintings, including Blue Boy, Olympia, and Toilers of The Sea.

"Well — thank you — enjoy yourself. I love that dress; is that a Christian Perrin Design? She is a real genius!" Constance said looking over and realizing she was the one woman more beautiful than herself, and she felt a little inferior.

"Yes, it is, and it was a gift after an interview with her," Rose said, still amazed by all the glitter. She stopped to see the singer get introduced just as Charleton saw ex-Governor and now Senator from Missouri, Kit Bond, who moved toward the orchestra. "Excuse me ladies, I must talk to Senator Bond."

Constance ignored this and said to Miss LaVon, "Good luck tonight if you get to talk to him, he's too busy hob-knobbing. Oh, have you heard Phyllis DeJayne sing? She's wonderful," Constance said as she turned toward the singer, smiling graciously through her introduction by the conductor, she then belted out George Gershwin's "Embraceable You," which was one of Constance's favorite songs. She was so happy she was singing it she couldn't help but smile. The song was done so well, it seemed George had written it just for her.

"Wasn't that great Mrs. Magenta? She's going places," Rose said, clapping loudly.

"Call me Constance, and yes, she is. Hey, you just mingle. If you need anything let me know. I must go say 'hi' to an old friend," Constance said, patting Rose on the arm, she left quietly.

Constance went toward an older woman sitting in the corner of the room on a white and brown fainting couch. She was dressed in an older gown, well maintained which had high shoulders draped by an old fur collar. She was also wearing a hat with feathers and pearls in it, much too gaudy for this occasion. It covered her thin white hair, revealing a pink scalp with freckles. She was a little heavy, lots of wrinkles and liver spots on her face; she wore glasses that made her eyes look big. She was sitting alone with her old wooden cane, crooked and varnished. She was enjoying watching the younger folks dance and mingle as she sipped tea. This was Madame Kendell, the only true aristocrat there, having been born in Britain.

"Hi Madame Kendell, it's great to see you again; you look like you're really enjoying yourself," Constance said as she leaned to embrace her tightly. Madame Kendell did the same, smiling — showing all the less than white teeth she still had. "A great party, love, you do know how to make everyone feel welcome. This one's almost as good as the one I attended at Blenheim Palace. The music, the food, all excellent, and that girl can really sing. She should be on Broadway."

"Yes, she will be someday, I'm sure." Constance said as she sat beside the old lady whose fragrance was filtered with Ben-Gay, she being in her eighties now.

"Are you all right, Love? I've been watching you and you seem a little down. Your husband's scarcely been around you five minutes. I'll listen if you want to bare your heart to this old bird." (She called everyone she dearly liked 'Love', whether they were British or American.)

"Oh, Madame Kendell, you've always been a great listener. Ever since we moved into this neighborhood five years ago, you truly have been so kind to me. I guess I didn't know next door neighbors could be such good friends." Constance said, reflecting on the kindness the Madame had shown her; her listening ear had truly been the most valuable to her.

"Well, Love, I enjoy you so much especially since I lost my hubby six years ago. It's been a bit of a struggle to go on — oh my, she's singing, "I'M IN THE MOOD FOR LOVE," great, great! Anyway, before I moved out here, you came clear across town when George died to offer your help — when I felt so alone, that meant a lot to me. I know some in our circle just say, 'if you need something' just to sound sincere, but you mean it. All the meals and flowers; I won't ever forget that; but, Love, what's eating you? You seem so unhappy."

"I watched you tonight and it was the same way at the Women's Auxiliary meeting. Your mind just seemed a million miles away. Is Charleton gone too much? Or is it something else?" Madame Kendell said as she looked Constance in the face, seeing that far-away look again as she gazed into the crowd and stared right through them. She looked off in the distance through the large plate glass window and seemed to be cognizant of the entire estate. She could see the cars parked on the grounds, the statues of Venus de Milo, David and two children gathering water, to the front and off to the side they all seemed eerie in the full moonlight. Even the large marble steps which led to the concrete driveway seemed to be calling her.

Constance really felt that she wanted to just leave to go to a quieter, gentler place where she could be happy all the time. She totally spaced off Madame Kendall who was trying to grab her arm to get her attention; finally, Constance responded, "Oh what? I'm sorry, say what you were saying, she does sing very well. That's my favorite song of all time by Yip Harburg, "Somewhere Over the Rainbow why oh why can't I…"

Constance continued to sing to herself as if they were floating in and out of her own world. She turned to Madame Kendell and said, "Don't you ever wish you could just fly over the rainbow, to just break away and be in a world that everyone cared about you; where you could be in a place that your husband only thought about you? In a place that you knew beyond a shadow of doubt that he only wanted you?"

Madame Kendell looked up, squinting through her failing eyes, she said softly, "Constance I do understand, and it does mean something to have your husband only want you, to only love you. You know, Love, back in Dover when my husband was a young man, he loved soccer, that was his chief passion. He ate, slept and drank soccer. I had Nellie, Sam and Jake, who was only eight years of age. He ignored us, he didn't seem to care. I finally got tired. I told him he jolly well better take care of his family or else. I really gave him a what for and he'd better straighten up or he'd end up in the boot or he'd be smashed on my windscreen. I mean he married me, not a game that I never really liked. Men, they can be awfully strange at times."

"He finally got the picture. He finally realized that his family came first. American men, they still leave a lot to be desired especially during football season. However, the best of them realize 'if Mummy ain't happy, ain't nobody happy.' Why do men put us on the back burner? I just don't get it."

"Love, you've got everything a woman could ever want, wealth, power, respect, and a husband that loves you. Sometimes you just need to sit down and count your blessings. There are a lot of women out there that would love to be in your shoes." Madame Kendell said, wondering if she was getting her point across. Just then, everyone heard the deep booming voice of Charleton calling

Constance to the platform in front of the piano. He was speaking loudly letting everyone know he had some great news to share. The time had come.

Constance saw her husband stand well above the microphone on the platform. He bent over and raised it up to his height. She noticed that he did look happy as she made her way through the sea of bodies. She also noticed he seemed to stare a little too long at Rose, who was standing quietly to the right of the harp musician.

"Ladies and gentlemen, here she comes, the most beautiful lady in the whole world," Charleton said, stretching his arms out to welcome his wife. He noticed she walked slowly toward him as if she was unsure about all of this. He pulled her gently onto the wooden platform.

Constance waved and smiled as her husband bent over and kissed her on the right cheek. Then he continued, "I hope everyone has enjoyed themselves tonight. The orchestra has been phenomenal and Miss DeJayne, what more can we say about her but a star is born."

"It is so good to see old friends and colleagues, to see former Governor's Kit Bond and Joe Teasdale and it's great to see you all. My son Ted and my daughter Teresa could not be here; they send their regards."

"I gathered you all here to make a special announcement. As most of you know, the slogan of my company is 'To Build A Better Way'. Well, taking a clue from that and looking at the way our country and state have changed, I believe it's time for me to try and build a better world. So, with the whole-hearted support of my family, I say this, Babe, how would you like to be the new First Lady of the great State of Missouri and me the next Governor?"

"Yes, I, Charleton Magenta, officially throw my hat into the ring to be your next Governor in 2004!" he blurted out loudly. The crowd erupted into cheers and applause throughout the entire estate as his voice boomed through the sound system. Everyone thought this was a fabulous idea, everyone except Constance. She stood on the platform dumbfounded as she watched her husband jump off the platform and started to shake hands. The orchestra then struck up a hardy rendition of Stars and Stripes Forever. Stunned, Constance started to cry. Unsure of what to do and realizing she had zero desire to be the First Lady of this state or any other state. She finally yelled, knowing that, in public, she should keep a more stoic demeanor; but she felt she couldn't now. He had trampled on her again. "No, no! How could you do this without talking to me? I hate you! You don't care about me at all. I just can't take it anymore," Constance said crying and mumbling into the microphone, but everyone at the party heard her mumble something but they weren't sure what. Constance was shaking so hard. She felt everyone staring at her, but she just didn't care anymore. Her emotional dam had burst.

The crowd around her at first was too caught up in the hand shaking, back patting and the general frivolity of the moment and didn't seem to notice, especially the men. The sensitivity of the women caused them to be drawn to the tears and there was a mumbling in the crowd as women began to say, "What's wrong with Constance?" With this came a crescendo of amazement that filled the room, and everyone turned toward the platform as the music stopped unevenly.

Charleton finally sensing a stirring that didn't involve him saw everyone looking toward the platform. He ran back towards his wife and as he did, she put her shaky hands out to keep him away. Then she screamed "No! Don't touch me, don't! How many times will you hurt me?! I can't be perfect anymore, no more, I can't be. I'm a human being not a Barbie doll. You won't even talk to me. You don't care a thing about me. I've got to get out of here. I have to!" with that Constance jumped off the platform and started to run, someplace, anyplace.

"What?" Charleton was awed by all of this, embarrassed, feeling ridiculed and tarnished socially, politically and as a man. He motioned for the orchestra to resume but no music began as his jaw dropped at this revelation. However, being a man of quick wit in difficult situations, he said "folks she's had a long day. She doesn't know what she's saying. She planned this entire party, what a lady, eh? Orchestra: Stars and Stripes, c'mon," he said with a broken smile, trying to ease those in attendance. The mood in the room had definitely changed: his moment had slipped away like a brief rain in parched earth — wondering if it had really rained at all. The orchestra slowly started again. It could hardly be heard above all the mumbling, murmurings and questions.

Charleton caught up with Constance and grabbed her from the back, twisting her around so, for a moment they were face to face. Her makeup now a runny mess, like a bad oil painting, he whispered, "What are you doing? We're in public, act like it. Don't embarrass me. Shush" he said as quietly as he could. "Embarrass you? Let go of me! You just don't get it! Charleton the skyscraper king! The master highway builder! You can't even build a driveway to my heart, let me go! I have to get out of here! Don't, don't touch me anymore, I hate you, oh how I hate you!" Constance yelled loudly as if she wanted the whole world to know how she felt.

"Come back here! You can't leave me!" Charleton yelled as he chased his wife through the crowd. He continued to grow angrier, upset and stupefied by the whole situation. Constance ran as fast as she could, knocking the servers and her guests out of her way unconcerned for their safety. She lost track of her husband and everyone else. She just had to get away; she kept yelling, "I have to get away! He beats me! I have to get away!" Completely unaware of obstacles seen or unseen, she ran toward the front of the Great Room. She saw the large plate glass window, perhaps seeing or not really seeing it as a window or perhaps as some sort of a door. "Yes" she said out loud, "Yes, my way out. God has provided my way out" getting closer to it, unaware of her actions as if her whole life was totally swallowed up by a flood that now engulfed her; she jumped high into the air and shattered the plate glass window into a thousand pieces, falling like tinsel onto the hedges below.

Part II

Chapter 7

Could it indeed have been the providence of God that had protected Constance that night? Because only God himself knows why she only received mild lacerations to her legs, arms, neck and face, which had to have stitches that created a curious design just under her left eye. Her body had received bruises from the hedges below. Everyone agreed that if the bushes hadn't been there a shard of glass may have ended up in her heart or sliced her aorta. Her survival could only be deemed a miracle.

The ambulance that had been called took her to the University Medical Center where she requested and received a private room. She was hooked up to an IV machine and had bandages on her head, face, arms and legs. The nurses came in to take her temperature and blood pressure regularly. Though her husband had rode in the ambulance with her, it was thought best by Doc Ellis that she should rest alone through the night; so he slept in the waiting room.

At 7:00am Doc Ellis entered Constance's room which was painted white with a TV near the ceiling and a table and chairs near the tall window. The Doc came with his nurses and awakened her.

"Constance, good morning, don't cha know."

Constance heard the voices but saw no one at first. Then she slowly opened her eyes. Her face was swollen and achy, along with the rest of her body.

"How are you doing Constance, don't cha know?" Doc Ellis asked, wearing his usual white coat with a stethoscope in his coat pocket.

"Oh, hi, where am I?" Constance said slowly seeing their faces as she looked around at the chrome and vinyl, which told her where she was.

"At the Med Center, we brought you here about 8:30 last night, don't cha know. Do you remember anything, don't cha know." Doc Ellis said, leaning over the hospital bed. Using a small light, he looked into her eyes and ears.

"Here, here," Constance, still incoherent, pushed the bed control and raised her bed some, "water" she added.

Her nurse, very heavy but smiling, wearing white shoes and hose, got her a foam cup of water with a bent straw and gave it to Constance. She took a strong sip.

"You're at the University Med Center, don't cha know. Other than a few bumps, bruises and scrapes, you should have a full recovery, don't cha know." Doc Ellis said, looking at her then at her chart.

"Scrapes, bruises? What happened?" Constance asked, starting to look at her body and seeing all the bandages. She felt them around her cheeks and eyes.

"You honestly don't remember crying, running and trying to hurdle the picture window in the Great Room?" Doc Ellis asked shocked that she was unaware of her plight. He watched her struggle to remember as she squinted, he continued, "look, we'll discuss this later, don't you know." Doc Ellis smiled as he put his hands on hers, turning, he mumbled something to his nurse, then left.

Constance leaned back against her extra soft pillows. She looked at her IV machine. Her hand, where all the lines of the IV machine were attached, her memory still seemed cloudy. She tried to recall how she was relatively enjoying the party, until the announcement came about her being the First Lady. It had hit her hard mainly because it hadn't been discussed between her and her husband. She felt it should have been. She remembered it was Charleton who chose the wedding colors of white and gold. It was Charleton who chose to honeymoon in Branson, Missouri. It was Charleton who named the children, Charleton; she knew, did everything except bear the children and take care of things at the estate day to day.

As she laid there in the solitude of early morning, her memory slowly started to come back, especially the reason she was so unhappy. She just felt neglected, to the point the love for her husband was starting to turn to hate. She knew she didn't really hate her husband, in fact, she knew deep down, she really did love him. She reflected on when her husband had advertised for a secretary to help at his office when he was just starting out and she had just finished secretarial training at Stephens College. She applied for the position, and she was hired.

Constance thought how kind he was when she worked there, he was always calling to check in or to take her out to lunch. He never seemed too busy for her, even on a work level. After a few months they began to see each other socially. Then at the end of their first year together as a couple they were married. Even then Charleton was so kind. Whenever he came home from building decks or pouring sidewalks, they would spend hours just loving on each other. They argued very little, but after the fifth year of being in business, it exploded to the point that she didn't have to work full time. Besides having Teresa, her daughter, a few years later, she became pregnant with Ted. Her job was now all domestic. The thing she remembered most was the change in Charleton. He seemed to grow darker all the time. He didn't want to make love all night anymore. He didn't have time for her anymore. Making money seemed more important to him. Yes, she knew as the money got better so did the houses and cars, but their relationship got worse. She just wanted him! Constance took another sip of water after retrieving her cup from a small table that held a slim dial telephone, and a small beige plastic pitcher of water. She looked outside only to see other buildings but no people.

She began to remember the night he asked her to marry him. Her soon-to-be-husband had taken her for a drive twenty miles Northeast of Columbia. They turned off the Harrisburg blacktop onto an old gravel road and then onto a hill where at night you could see all the lights of Columbia at one time.

They were driving his fathers '53 Chevy pickup, which was a real beater; it used a gallon of oil a trip. It was late but Charleton had said he had a big announcement to make. Constance knew then she was really in love with him. He was handsome and had a future in front of him.

Constance watched him closely that night as he said, "Babe, it's been almost a year now, and well, I'm really not the best at this. I really do love you and I want you to be my wife. I can't promise you riches right now, but I promise you I will always cherish you. I will never put anything above you. You will be my all in all. You know I ain't much with fancy words, but I heard a fella say that cherish is really two words in one; 'Chair' like a La-Z-Boy, that your wife should be treated like a Queen all the time. The chair is her throne and 'ish' means wish, that her wishes should all come true, that the man should make her every wish come true. Babe, if you marry me, I will do my best to make that happen." Constance smiled at this thought realizing that she indeed said "yes" to him that day, but her wishes hadn't come true, at least not all of them. Before she could finish her reflection, her breakfast came. The attendant dressed in blue and wearing a hairnet didn't speak. She sat the tray down on the adjustable table, rolled it over and adjusted it so Constance could eat. She realized she was a little hungry.

It wasn't fifteen minutes later that her husband arrived shabbily dressed with beard stubble, looking like he hadn't slept all-night, though he had combed his hair. She saw him enter, but her feelings clouded by her reverie. She seemed content to see him for the moment.

"Babe, are you okay?" Charleton said genuinely concerned for her. He felt her pain after seeing all her bandages again this morning.

"Okay why does everybody keep asking me that? You'd think I did something really stupid. Doc Ellis mentioned something about a plate glass window. Here, do you want my orange juice?" Constance asked, offering the small unopened, ribbed container to her husband.

"No thanks. You honestly don't remember what happened?" Charleton asked, realizing she might have amnesia or perhaps be blocking it out. He thought it might be best if he concentrated on her physical health for now. "Babe, I met Doc Ellison on the way from the elevators; he said you could probably go home tomorrow."

"That's good; I hate hospitals. Too much Lysol for me," Constance said, seemingly lost in another world but coming back to her present one. "You know, you really should shave."

"I know. I was just anxious to see you. I stayed here all night. Babe, I really do love you. Funny on the way over here, I just kept thinking about the first day we met. I mean I really didn't believe in love at first sight, but it was in your case. When I first saw you, it was like seeing the biggest diamond in the world behind a plate glass display case. You sparkled like something I've never seen, my heart just seemed to overflow like Niagara Falls."

Constance just mumbled back to her husband as if those words, plate glass, suddenly prompted a vail to lift; and suddenly, the whole morbid scene came back to her. She saw herself running towards the large window in the Great Room screaming, "I've got to get out of here!" The words played over and over again in her mind like a bad movie. It prompted her without warning to start screaming the same words.

Charleton jumped back, startled by this outburst as the nurse entered hearing the screaming also. Constance screamed even louder as the nurse tried to calm her, "I've got to get out of here. Don't touch me! Charleton never touch me again! Get out of here! I don't want to see you again - ever!"

"Mrs. Magenta, calm down, you're fine," her nurse said, putting her arms across Constance's shoulders to try to restrain her. Constance started to twitch, pulling the IV out of her hand causing blood to drip onto the floor. She knocked her breakfast tray table over, causing her food to spill everywhere.

Her nurse pushed the call button on the arm of the bed to get more help. Charleton looked on in disbelief as his wife continued to scream, "I hate you Charleton! I hate you! I've got to get out of here!" over and over again.

Chapter 8

Charleton was sitting in the visitors lounge when he saw his son Teddy walk past, he called over to him, "Teddy, over here."

Teddy turned around to find the room fairly busy for a Saturday. Both TVs were on and hanging from the ceiling. Some kids, one with a broken arm, were playing with oversized LEGO's and many were reading old issues of popular magazines.

"How was your flight from Seattle?"

"Fine and mom, is she alright?" Teddy asked quietly. His father motioned for him to sit across from him on a plaid cushioned chair with shiny wooden arms. He did as he was told and continued, "Dad it's all over the news, CNN, Fox Network, Newspapers, what's going on? The reporters are all over the place downstairs. It's good that security isn't letting them come up here. I had to sneak in the back entrance. They're calling mom crazy, unstable, unfit to be the First Lady. What's that about? They say you're running for Governor. Is that true?"

"Yeah, I am, that was the big announcement. I guess I should have talked this over with your mother first and you and your sister too," Charleton said, putting his head in his hands in regret.

"What? You mean you didn't discuss it with mom at all? Come on dad! Melissa would have killed me if I'd have done that to her. They are saying mom was screaming and intentionally tried to jump through the plate glass window. What's going on?" Teddy asked, pretty disturbed at all this.

"Son, I guess I was wrong in not telling her and you and your sister. I just figured she'd be happy for me and happy for herself," Charleton said through tearing eyes, trying more to convince himself than his son.

"I just can't believe it! You know dad, I don't get you sometimes. I mean, you can run a Fortune 500 company so well but when it comes to mom, you haven't got a clue. They said at the party she was yelling 'I got to get away, I got to'," Teddy paused, then he whispered, "The news said, she screamed something about you beating her."

"Beat her? Son, we have our fights like most couples do, I never beat her." Charleton said softly to his son as if he didn't want anyone around them to hear. The same reason he figured Ted had whispered to him.

"Dad, I hope not! What about her saying she just had to get away? Get away from what?" Ted said while getting up and shaking his head at even the thought of what his mother just went through.

"I don't know son, I really don't know what's going on with her right now. Maybe she just needs a vacation," he said sniffling a bit realizing he really knew much more than what he was sharing.

"What room is she in?" Ted asked, looking at his father grow emotional, something he rarely did unless he was angry.

"Room 83, turn right at the nurse's station, second room on the left. Go ahead, I'll visit later. I'm sure she'd like to see you," Charleton said, waving. As Ted started out of the lounge he turned around and said, "Dad we need to talk. Oh, Teresa will be in late tonight. I called her to let her know what was going on." Then he left after he saw his dad nod back, "fine."

Charleton sat quietly wondering if anyone heard his whisper about "beating his wife." He knew according to him he never beat her, but he also knew occasionally their fights became physical. He knew he had a temper.

"If she would just do what I say and stop whining, everything would be okay." He said to himself.

Charleton took a handkerchief from the back pocket of his tux he was still wearing from the night before. He dried his tears, blew his nose, and then he leaned back in his chair wondering what really caused his wife to seemingly have a mental breakdown.

Yes, he knew he didn't control his temper very well, like the time he came home from work when the kids were small, the house was a wreck and there was no dinner ready. He had accused his wife of being a lazy bum. He had slapped her hard on the face. He later apologized profusely that he got a babysitter and took his wife out on the town to make up for his contemptible behavior.

He also thought about the time she cooked his steak too well done, he went berserk, throwing things, hitting her in the ribs, cracking two.

He shook his head again as if he was trying to rid his mind of such a horrible memory. Before this could happen, a young man with spiked pink hair, a nose ring and a ring above his right eye had just entered the room. He obviously had looked at the TV above him and not liking "Barney" he reached up and began to change the channel. He stopped briefly on CNN to see the news of the day scroll across the bottom of the screen while a female reporter with long black hair and a serious face was saying, "I'm standing in front of the gates of the Magenta mansion here in Columbia, Missouri where last night a gala was held for the announcement of Charleton Magenta the Billionaire and President of Magenta Inc., the biggest construction company in a five state area announced his run for Governor, 2004. Witnesses say his wife, Constance Magenta, ran out of the mansion upon hearing this announcement screaming like a mad woman. The reason is unclear at this time. She tried to jump through a large window and succeeded. Her fall was broken by the hedges below, which some say saved her life. As you see the gates are locked and only the police are going in and out. So many awful things were said too. Here with me is Gertrude Ellis, the wife of Doc Ellis, who is currently treating Mrs. Magenta. She agreed to speak with us today. Mrs. Ellis was in attendance at the gala turned tragedy last night."

"Can you tell us what happened here last night Mrs. Ellis?" asked the reporter as she put a large round microphone that looked like a black and silver ice cream cone in front of her.

"It's really hard to tell. My husband and I have been friends with the Magenta's for years. Never have I seen anything like this! I mean, they never ever fought or even argued in public. Once in a while Charleton would tease her in public, nothing that I felt out of the ordinary though. I can't say what went on behind closed doors. I guess what set her off was evidently that Charleton never consulted her on the idea of being the First Lady. That would hurt me too. Constance is a fine woman." Gertrude said honestly. She was dressed in a soft summer outfit of brown with her hair rolled up making her look younger than she was.

"What do you think she meant by, 'I've got to get away?' What do you think she was running from and what was she saying about her husband beating her? What do you know about all that?" the reporter asked, cringing on the thought of any woman being beaten.

"Beating, I don't know but Charleton seems to treat her well, at least every time I've seen them in public. What she's running from, I'm not sure, but …" Gertrude paused as if not wanting to say anything more. The reporter caught this hesitation.

"Go on," the reporter urged.

"Well, my husband has been their family physician for over twenty-five years, he's often told me about questionable injuries she had …"

"Questionable? Like what?"

"Look, can we talk about something else? They're a fine couple." Gertrude said, swallowing hard.

"Yes, if you wish. However, I must ask, is he fit? Is she fit? Are they fit to be our next Governor and First Lady in your opinion?"

The pink headed young man became bored and turned the channel much to the relief of Charleton. He mumbled to himself, "Gertrude is a traitor, talking to the world about my wife and me. I hope nobody notices me. Unfit, fit to be Governor, you bet. Questionable injuries, what's that all about? Man, it seems like suddenly everyone is against me."

Finally, he got up as he felt everyone stare at him, like he had committed a great sin. He started to walk out of the lounge when the pink headed man started to walk out too. The young man stared at him as if he knew him, then spoke, "Hey, aren't you the CEO of Magenta Inc.? I just purchased 50 shares of your stock, keep the price up. The press, they are all a bunch of vultures." Then he reached out his hand and Charleton shook it.

"Yes, thank you for having faith in our company. Who might you be?" Charleton said, unsure of what to think of this exchange.

"K.T., third year business student at M.U. hey, I know a lot of people stare at me but it's not what's on the outside that counts, it's what's on the inside," K.T. said, rather stoically, "my fiancée is in here for a broken arm. Take care."

"Yes, I will K.T. thanks." Charleton watched the young man go in a different direction, realizing that his outward appearance was awful, but he seemed at peace with himself, something he knew he wasn't.

Chapter 9

Ted had talked to his mother at the hospital and found her tired and rambling. He felt his dad really didn't care enough about her, this had been evident for years and for some reason it showed at the hospital.

He knew materially dad was an excellent provider, but he seemed not to care at all about his mother's emotional welfare, that somehow he had shut her out of his life.

Ted knew ever since he could remember, he ignored her at social gatherings because he was too busy making connections for his next business venture, but he made sure no one there was dressed more elegantly than her, and she was always the most beautiful.

Everyone in town knew they were the perfect couple, even though at times he could be coarse in public. Like the time they went bowling for the local "March of Dimes" and she bowled 100. He chided her in front of everyone, saying "Babe, a pet monkey could bowl better than you!" Everyone looked at him strangely for that comment. When he started to laugh, everyone did also, except his mother, sister and himself. He was twelve at the time and his sister was fifteen.

As Ted grew older and his dad grew richer, his mother just got prettier she had more baubles and the whole family lived better.

Whenever they traveled, they only stayed in five-star hotels, eating the best foods, getting the best seats on airplanes, before they eventually purchased their own plane. Ted liked this luxury, but he was still often disturbed that his mother wasn't treated better.

He felt like at times his father treated her like a sex object and nothing more. Although there were times of frivolity, they didn't last long.

Ted felt that he didn't really understand women either. All he knew was the prettier the better. Deep down inside he knew there had to be more important issues about loving a woman.

As he watched his mom sleeping in her hospital bed with all the machines attached to her and all the bandages, he hurt for her. He knew he really loved her because it was his mother that taught him patience. It was his mother who pitched the baseball around in the backyard. She was the one that played hide and seek, Ollie, Ollie Oxen Free, Red Light-Green Light and Mother, May I with him and his sister, Teresa. It was his mother who attended all the school functions. On occasion his father would make a guest appearance at the PTA meetings.

"Where was he?" Ted wondered about his dad, but he knew he was out building his empire. He was always out getting more projects and making more money. He was no doubt a workaholic, which Ted followed in his father's footsteps on that issue, but he tried overall to treat women in his life better than his dad did.

He had in recent years dated Tonya Green, but he found her plain, slightly dense and lacking in the better breeding most of his other girlfriends had, especially like Melissa who he had been dating for the last two-and-a-half years.

Melissa had told him on their first date that she was a Francophone from Montreal, Canada. Her father was a purveyor in precious metals and her mother worked at Centre d'Histoire de Montreal. It was after her real mother had died when she was five that her dad married an American socialite from Washington DC who was heavily into arts, literature and culture, who thought every little girl should be, bred a lady so her sole aim after marrying Melissa's father had been to make her the next Jacqueline Bouvier Kennedy. She had no children of her own and Melissa was an only child so makeup, parties, beauty pageants and modeling were her only life.

Melissa told Ted she knew more about makeup at seven than most women do at twenty-one. Though she always looked great and spoke properly, she could be very moody at times; they got along so well that they were planning on getting married next June.

He did love her, and he had decided after hearing all the negative reports about the party, and the press calling his father an abuser and calling his mother crazy — all of which hurt him deeply — to think long and hard about what a family should be.

Yes, he knew his father wasn't the kindest father on the block. He was tough but also fair. He would defend you until the last bullet flew. Ted knew this early on, when a boy at school stole his bike. His father personally came to school, settling the issue and making it very plain that no one messed with his kid. Why, once he had watched his sister being escorted to the door by one of her boyfriends who seemed to get too friendly; Teresa screamed, dad came to the door and told the boy, "You put your hands on my daughter, I'll put my hands on you, got it?" That put an end to any guys treating his sister badly.

For Ted, family was important and as he was driving home from visiting his mother, he though not a religious person, was for some reason starting to think about the way his father treated his mother more and more. He knew Melissa was a prize catch. She was on the covers of ELLE, Vogue, MS Magazine, and many others.

She was a spokesmodel for car companies, drink products and lately for her dad's new restaurant chain he just opened up, which is how they met. They had hit it off quickly and soon she became his best friend.

As he pulled into the driveway of his townhouse, he looked up to see Melissa's outline in the upstairs bedroom, even her silhouette looked beautiful as he watched her for a moment. This idea of family made him realize that their living together maybe wasn't the best thing, but he reasoned, "What the heck, most couples do it anyway."

Even though he knew it was wrong by his compulsory church attendance until the age of 16, the idea of living with your future wife really didn't seem to be a great sin compared to other really bad sins. Ted thought, "I love her, isn't that enough," as he got out of his Lexus, staring at her silhouette again and sighed, "What a looker!"

CHAPTER 10

Constance was released early Monday morning. She was given a few prescriptions to calm her nerves and help her sleep. Her daughter finally arrived from Australia late Sunday night and had stayed at the Estate. She had come by herself.

It was around 10:00 am when she got to see her mother. Teresa was fair-haired, a little heavier than her mother and not quite as pretty and a little more straightforward like her father. She was married to a preacher, and she ran an Internet site for women who were hurting. Teresa was impeccably dressed. The only real perk she claimed from her wealthy family was that she took pride in the family name, and she felt that wealth was meant to bless others. She was never unkind and always spoke the truth. She was wearing soft jeans and a T-shirt that said 'W.W.J.D.' She sat quietly in a low back, wooden chair with a soft cushion as she held her mother's hand in the glow of the light of the master bedroom.

"Mother, it's your Teresa. I'm here now. I got in late last night. I called Dad and he thought it was best if I just waited for you here. Are you all right?" Teresa asked quietly while watching her mother stir a little out of an uncomfortable sleep.

"Teresa, oh hi, Ted told me you were coming. How's Edward? Did he come too? And the kids?" Constance asked, breathing a little heavy.

"No, he's preaching a revival starting tonight in CanBerra. He really wanted to come, but I told him I'd just go this time. He's so understanding. The kids send you kisses." Teresa said, reaching to brush some hair from her mother's face, she continued, "Mom, what happened? The news networks are saying a lot of crazy things about you."

"Like what? I guess I've been a little out of it. I haven't paid much attention," Constance said, trying to sit up in bed. Teresa quickly adjusted her pillows.

"Would you like something to drink? Here, have a little iced tea." Teresa sat down and gave her mom a sip through a long red straw.

"That tastes so good, a little more sugar, please," Constance said watching her daughter shake the sugar packet then tear the top off. She then stirred it into the tea with an iced-tea spoon. She gave her mother another sip.

"Daddy didn't cause you to do this did he? Governor, did he even ask you about it, one time? He never talked with me or Ted about the decision to run for Governor. First time I heard about it was on the news." Teresa said, noticing her mother become a little more relaxed.

Constance shook her head 'no' to both questions.

"C'mon mother, why do you deny what he's done to you over the years? Mother, I really do love you and dad both, but no woman has to stay with an abusive husband."

"Abusive? What are you talking about? Your father never touched me! I mean every couple fights a little, you know that. Haven't you and your hubby, Edward ever fought?" Constance said, watching Teresa get up and walk around as if she was very disturbed at this response.

"Mother I don't believe that at all, fighting between married couples isn't in the Bible. Edward and I decided that we would not argue or fight. We would instead be mature and discuss our differences like two adults should be able to. Could you even imagine Jesus the Son fighting God the Father?"

"Mother, you are the greatest woman I know. You're beautiful on the outside and you're beautiful on the inside. I'm so glad you're my mother — but do you really think Ted and I never heard you arguing? Or we never heard of things being thrown or broken? Do you think we never wondered why, at the dinner table, you were wearing sunglasses? Mother, we both knew, dad hit you. We both knew that he called you stupid and the "B" word at home. I know this is probably tough to hear right now, but I care about you. I don't want you abused anymore. How much more are you going to take? Mother, I don't want to see you end up a statistic."

"Too many abused women end up scarred for life. They end up in a vicious cycle of being abused over and over again by their partner, who says, 'Oh honey, I won't do it again, I promise,' but then something else ticks them off and then the cycle starts all over again and some, I know this won't sound good, but some husbands even end up killing their wives — the woman they promised to love and cherish forever and ever, 'to death do us part.'"

"Mother, even before this happened, half a world away, I woke up in the middle of the night. I really felt God telling me to pray for you and I did all night. I want to see you happy and well. It seems like every time I come to visit it's a crisis. Just remember this: the person who angers you is the person who controls you."

"How long, Mother, are you going to resist God? He doesn't want you to live like this! No woman deserves to be beaten and abused, no woman, enough is enough!" Teresa said, leaning over and hugging her mother gently. She said nothing as if in deep thought, reflecting on the harsh reality that was just shared.

"Mother, look, this is an option; you are welcome to live with us for a while so you can get things sorted out. I know you have a lot of years with dad. Being married over thirty-three years is great, but I just wonder how many moments, hours and days you lived in fear that he was going to lash out at you again. You just can't continue to live this way."

"I haven't talked with daddy yet about this issue, but something has to change; it has to!"

Chapter 11

At 8:00 am a temporary nurse was at the Estate to look after Constance; while Frances attended to her normal duties, Teresa decided to stay in town for a few extra days to comfort her mother. Charleton decided that, for his own mental stability, he needed to go to work and maintain his usual routine.

As his chauffeur Joe drove up past his Atlas fountain, right at the entrance, reporters from CNN, Fox, KOMU-TV, KCRG, BBC and other news outlets were just waiting for him with microphones and TV cameras right in his face. As he exited his limo, not yet standing, they started to hound him, "Mr. Magenta, would you care to make a statement on what your chances for becoming Governor are in light of all that has happened?"

"And what about your wife, is she unstable: why did she jump through the window? How long has she been like this — to do what she did? The public has a right to know. And what about her saying you beat her? Is that true?"

"Aw-gee, would you stop asking me questions! I'll have a press conference later."

Charleton shook his head wishing all the journalists would just disappear. He finally made it to the large glass doors leading into the building as they were still following him. He became fed up with them. He turned and blurted out "I want to remind you all this is private property, and if you don't leave, I'll call the proper authorities." They finally backed off.

Ellie, his secretary, watched Charleton enter the building. She, along with some of his other employees, were watching this display from the hallway looking outside, "Get to work all of you! I don't pay you to stand around and gawk!" Charleton shouted at them. When he entered, they all scattered to their offices, that's when he noticed Rose sitting quietly in the hallway just past the coat rack next to the bottled water fountain. She was dressed in a soft red outfit. She seemed as refreshing as a blade of grass shooting through a slab of concrete. "Hey, how come you're not out there hounding me like the rest of your cohorts?" Charleton said as he slowly walked toward her. She got up to meet him.

"Because I'm a lady and true ladies don't hound, besides I still need my story, and I figure right now you could probably use a friend in the press."

"You're right there, Rose."

"Oh, Mr. Magenta, sir, Mr. Cox called, he's ready to deal on that project in Sedalia. He'd like to see you at the sight as soon as you can get there," Elle said.

"Fine, I'll go now. Oh Rose, our interview. Well maybe we can kill two birds with one stone. Listen, do you have time to go with me? We'll probably be gone for three or four hours," he said, pulling his cell phone out searching for Mr. Cox's number.

"Yes, I don't see a problem," Rose said smiling, showing her beautiful teeth.

"Hey, Elle, call Joe. Tell him to drive the car around to the side door. Maybe I can at least depart in peace," Charleton said, nodding for Rose to follow him. She followed with her small digital recorder in hand.

Charleton called Mr. Cox on the way down the hall, as he saw Joe drive up to the glass doors on the North side of the building. He could see the sun shining through as they exited the building.

Charleton opened the door for Rose, then he got in and said, "Joe, take us to Cox Industries in Sedalia. Joe, this is Miss Rose LaVon, a reporter, but she's a friendly one." Joe just smiled back in the rear-view mirror with his narrow clean-shaven face.

The limo eventually hit I-70 West. Rose looked around, liking the softness of the white button tufted leather seats and door panels. She noticed the TV, wet bar, sink and refrigerator.

"This is nice!"

"Yeah, it'll do — my little home away from home. Would you like a drink? I've got the hard stuff or soda."

"A Pepsi is fine."

"Okay," Charleton said as he reached over to get her a glass.

Rose thanked him by mouthing the words, "thank you."

"Well, tell me one thing, why is the press trying to make me out to be some kind of monster?" Charleton asked, turning toward her, trying to avoid looking at her shapely legs that were crossed, like a lady's should be.

"Shame, really. Bad news seems to always get the lead, but I have to ask, why was your wife saying, 'I have to get away,' and the worst part is when she talked about you beating her. Here, wait, let me start my Sony," Rose said, putting her drink down in the front cup holder.

"No, I'm not here to discuss that. You wanted to know about me. You wanted to know my story, that's all you'll get today, or you'll get nothing." Charleton said growing a little disturbed at the line of questioning, especially the part about beating his wife.

"Fair enough, sorry. It's just that I've never seen anything like that in my life, Hollywood yes, but real life, no. Okay tell me how you ended up the success you are today." Rose asked softly, feeling he was hiding something and the reason he only wanted to talk about himself.

"You see, my grandfather emigrated from Poland. He was an engineer there. With his help, they designed the George Washington Bridge in New York in 1931, the G.W. is supposed to be the busiest bridge in the world. Well, he taught my father how to be a bridge builder too, which he did for most of his life. Eventually he switched to houses and I learned that from him, so here I am. My father however died when I was twenty-four years old, so I just continued his legacy, but I concentrated on decks, sidewalks, fences, and those sorts of things. I really wasn't into building houses, but I developed a reputation for excellent work. Now, thirty years later, it's entire subdivisions, factories, hotels, bridges, strip malls, and now highways. Cox Industries wants me to expand their warehouse another six hundred thousand square feet. That's where we're headed to discuss the proposal. Not a problem, we can do it." Charleton said leaning back, puffed up with pride.

"That's incredible. My research says you met Constance at work."

"Yes, I needed a secretary, she applied. We eventually fell in love and married. She really is a wonderful lady," Charleton said looking out the window wishing Constance was alright and sitting right beside him. "That's a great story in itself."

"How's the marriage been over the years? All the trades are saying you two were one of the most admired couples in the U.S." Rose asked, noticing that Charleton was no longer looking at her.

"It's fine. Eventually Constance will come around. I know she really does love me. She really doesn't want to run away from me. I made her what she is, you know." Charleton mumbled most of his response, except the last line and Rose heard it, which immediately struck her wrong; it sounded very chauvinistic.

"Really, just what do you mean by 'you made her what she is'," Rose asked in a very disturbed tone that only women really understand, but men get eventually.

"Look, it's a man's world. Women are just in it, that's all." Charleton said turning toward her, growing a little disturbed by these personal questions as he noticed her face grow quite upset.

"What do you mean it's a man's world; women are just in it? Do you think women are second class citizens?" Rose asked, her face growing flushed.

"No, but most of them would be better off staying home baking cookies and wiping noses. I really don't have a problem with women working but if their husband says no, she should listen to him. Even the Good Book says that men should rule over the women, right?"

"You got it all wrong. In Genesis Chapter 2, verse 18, it says, and I quote, 'and the Lord God said, It is not good that the man should be alone; I will make help and help meet for him,' unquote — the term help means helper, a suitable mate. One translation says, a teammate, and in the same chapter it says that woman was made from Adam's rib, from his side to be equal with. Mr. Magenta. I'm by no means a feminist, but I am appalled at your perspective on women." Rose said with a face as red as a checkerboard square.

"Sorry, I didn't mean to offend you, but women ought to stay out of a man's affairs. I've built an empire. I've taken care of my wife. She never has to want for anything. All of her clothes are custom designed. She can buy anything she could ever want with just a signature. You tell me if I'm such a rotten guy, the one she wants to run away from, why is she still there? Because I'm everything to her; without me she could do or be nothing. For all practical purposes I own Constance Magenta. I put her on the map," Charleton said smiling as he gloated over all he had accomplished. His face changed when he saw Rose's face grow redder and redder.

"Of all the unmitigated gall to think that you made anything. God alone is the Creator and He alone should be your all in all. Sir, I am a Christian. I've been one for over ten years now. My Lord Jesus means everything to me, and I would never have the guts to stick my finger in his face and say I did this, or I did that. Sir, I really caution you right now because the Bible says, and I quote, 'Pride goes before destruction and haughty spirit before a fall' unquote. So, you want to be the next Governor of Missouri, maybe, and I speak only as a friend, and I think I am one. Maybe you need to get your house in order first." Rose said boldly but with humility.

Charleton said nothing at first in response to this. Instead, he turned and looked outside the other window, sighed, wondering why he had asked her to come along in the first place. Obviously, she seemed to have a bone to pick with him too, so after the meeting with Cox Industries, where everything went well, Joe drove them back to Columbia. During the ride hardly a word was spoken between him and Rose. Joe drove Rose over to her car which was parked close to the front gate trying to avoid all the news networks who were still wanting a story about Charleton and his wife. They pressed their bodies and equipment right up against the side of the limousine. Joe made it to Roses car; he got out and he told her, "Goodbye," then he got back in to hear Charleton say, "Gee, Joe I'm glad we dropped her off. She's got a pretty face, great legs but a warped mind. Who does she think she is telling me to get my house in order, and that I am sticking my finger in God's face? Just take me home Joe." Charleton watched Joe smirk in the mirror wondering whether to speak, he rarely did, but this time he had felt particularly offended by Charleton's chauvinistic views for some reason. As a fairly new employee, he couldn't stand it anymore. His father had chauffeured the Magenta family for years before retiring when Joe took over just until his international banking career was established.

"Sir, may I take liberties and say something?" Joe asked, licking his lips, then adjusting his chauffeur's cap, which hid a mostly bald head.

"Go ahead. I hope you're not going to get on my case too. It seems lately everybody's out to get the rich kid on the block," Charleton said, reaching into the refrigerator and withdrawing a chilled wine cooler.

"Sir, normally I don't say much because I am paid to just drive you, but lately you've started to act like you built this empire, you alone, and women are just made to be used, like some, pardon the expression, like some party doll. You know Darcie and I celebrated our 25th wedding anniversary last spring and we are more in love than ever. We have mutual respect, one is not more important than the other, we're a team. I treat her like the Hope Diamond. That's how precious she is to me."

"So, what's the point, Joe?" Charleton said, interrupting him as he sipped on his wine cooler.

"The point is, Sir, I really don't like the way you treat women. On the surface you show them respect, but your eyes show disdain. I don't know how you can live with yourself some days, Sir. It's not a man's world; it belongs to God." Joe returned boldly, unusual for him, not flinching at all.

"Look, let's talk about something else. I do treat women well. I pay the highest salaries in the business. I was the first in town to have job sharing. I give personal sick days, an extra week of vacation for a job well done. What more do you want?"

"My wife is the wealthiest woman in the entire Midwest. She is the best dressed. There is nothing I wouldn't give her and ...."

"Excuse me Sir, things are nice, but do you give her love?" Joe asked, interrupting him.

"What in the world are you talking about, of course I love her!"

"Really, I took her to the salon last week. She cried all the way there and all the way back. She kept mumbling, 'I wish my husband would just love me, just love me. I wish he would just tell me I am his whole world,'" Joe said rather stoically looking in the mirror watching Charleton squirm a little.

"Really, look, I don't like this conversation. She knows I love her, why do I have to tell her? She knows she means the world to me, why do I have to tell her? Geez, I've heard enough. Just drive on." Charleton said smashing his body back into his limousine's plush leather seats. He took a final swig of his wine cooler and sighed wishing this day was over.

Chapter 12

Across town Tonya Green was putting her son Pookie to sleep in his animal painted youth bed right next to hers at her father's estate.

As she looked down on him, she realized what a blessing he was even though she hadn't planned on being a mother at eighteen. She had grandiose plans of being married first. Romance meant everything to her.

She was a modern-day Madame Bovary. She loved reading romance novels. Her favorite authors were Barbara Cartland, Nora Roberts, Catherine Cookson and Leo Tolstoy. Her favorite book was *Anna Karenina* — though she knew it was wrong, her favorite character was Count Vronsky. When, in fact, Levin or Alexandra Karenina would have been a better choice to emulate morally. The fact that Vronsky had swept Anna off her feet was breathtaking, while the tragedy at the end of the book always haunted her. She always wished they had a happier ending, but she knew that, starting a relationship illegitimately, made it difficult to be legitimized in the end.

However, now at age twenty-one, her naiveté seemed to be tempered by the reality of raising her son. She knew her mother had not been a very positive role model. She had not shown her or her sister, Amber, much love. She seemed to be lost in her own world; she was a hopeless romantic to the point she had become a Queen Bee. Her mother felt that a man was sent "only to serve" the woman and her philosophy was if she wasn't happy "no one else would be either." Tonya found this attitude to be very alarming because it made her father into a Casper Milk Toast which eventually led to their divorce. He finally developed a backbone, and he got tired of deriding him for not being more of a man. She was constantly criticizing him, cussing him out in public and private.

Tonya didn't like this at all, and she turned away from her mother and gravitated toward her father — who was a kind and gentle man who loved God and loved reaching out to others.

Her sister Amber gravitated toward her mother who was wild and unfaithful more than once — so Tonya and her mother didn't always get along — but she did love her.

As she watched her son sleep, she finally pulled the covers up around him then she just watched him sleep for a while, pursing his lips as children often do when having a good, peaceful dream. Tonya eventually pulled the silk covers back and crawled into bed with only a night light and the moonbeams gently streaming through the window; one fell on her son, the other across her bed, as if gently putting an arm across her, embracing her like an old friend.

As she rested quietly realizing how much her life had changed with Pookie, she couldn't help but think that God had used this child to get her attention. It just seemed like yesterday when she was pregnant and on the same day she found out she had a date with Ted. She really thought he would be happy because they had agreed on eventually having children.

Tonya remembered how stormy the day was; it seemed to rain all day, so after dinner they drove to a secluded spot north of town where the traffic was sparse, and they wouldn't be disturbed. She knew she had hinted all day about some big news and when the time came, she remembered saying, "Ted, I have some great news! I'm pregnant, we're gonna' have a baby."

Tonya remembered smiling but it quickly left as Ted said nothing. It was as if he was totally shocked then he hit the driver's side window with his fist and turned to her seething with anger. Tonya knew she would never forget his hate-filled words. "What!? I don't want no stinking kid right now! The kid will ruin everything for me! I'm set to graduate summa cum laude! This will totally mess up my life."

She had broken into tears as heavy as melting ice sickles after hearing these words; she tried to reason with him, "Ted, this is our child, part of you and me."

He didn't listen to that, he just yelled back, "So what! Kill it! I'll pay for an abortion. I don't need no stinking kid right now!" Those words, Tonya knew, still hurt her like a knife in her heart; she still tried to plead with him.

"Abortion? No way! You will love this child, you'll see! I know you will. We made him, you and me — in love."

Ted's response, "Shut up! Quit your crying! I've already told you twice. I don't want no stinking kid! You're so stupid! Can't you hear me talking to you? You don't listen, that's your problem, you're a dog, a real dog. I don't want to be around you anymore! No man will ever want you, no man! Get out of my car, get out of my life! You dog." Teddy responded that night full of anger by reaching across her lap and opening the door and shoving her out. At that moment the rain came down harder than it had all night.

Tonya remembered screaming, "No! Don't kick me out! I love you, Ted! I love you …." Before she could finish, she ended up in a rain filled ditch. All she could see were his taillights in the distance. She felt so cold, alone and dirty.

Tonya had tried to stand up but she had taken her shoes off and left them in Ted's car, thankfully, she'd wrapped her purse around her shoulder, which had her cell phone in it, which relieved her for a moment as a she sat in the mud with no shoes, the rain mixed with her heavy tears and sobs, she felt lost, forsaken and angry, wondering where she should go from here. Tonya looked up and with a loud voice she yelled, "God where are you? Where are you when I need you the most?" she slumped back down again.

She remembered crying for what seemed like days, when finally, a peace came over her that only God could have given her. An old Sunday school song started playing in her mind. "Jesus Loves Me this I know, for the Bible tells me so. Little ones to him belong, they are weak, but he is strong, yes, Jesus loves me. Yes, Jesus loves me."

With that, Tonya started to get up and then she got the strength to phone her father, who came quickly. She cried all the way home, resting on his shoulder.

Tonya remembered how her crying and the fact that her father found out the whole story and never judged her but instead he had accepted her, and he had just loved her for who she was, which helped her heal. She really loved her father for that.

Tonya smiled amazed at her father's love, which was the reason she had contacted Constance. Yes, now like everyone, she had heard the news about the tragic happening at Constance's estate, and Tonya was content to give Constance a little longer to respond to her letter, though she hoped the response would come soon.

Chapter 13

Though it was after 8:00 o'clock Monday evening, Teresa had called Ted and said that he needed to come by the Mansion so they both could talk to their father. They talked quite a while on just how they both felt, they knew it was time for them to confront their father.

The three of them (their father the only one dressed in pajamas—white and monogrammed), sat quietly in the family room with its white arching bookshelves with family photos on the shelves and black leather furniture with a large screen TV in the corner.

Charleton was sitting in his usual overstuffed chair and the children sat across from him. He was drinking scotch on the rocks; Ted had been the last to enter. He had looked in on his mother first.

"Mom looks better tonight," Ted said, looking at his father who seemed a bit jittery, obviously wishing this meeting was already over and wondering why he had agreed to it in the first place. He really didn't know.

"Yes, she does on the outside. Dad, we called you here to discuss some things. This isn't a slam party. We just want to know what's going on between you and mother," Teresa said as she stopped leafing through a Martha Stewart Magazine while watching her dad sit down, not interested in talking about anything, especially this issue. She sat the magazine on a hand painted glass coffee table.

Charleton took another swig of his liquor; then said rather sarcastically, "I bet the way you're both looking at me you think I threw your mom out the window."

"Absurd, really, tell me at the hospital why the nurses said mom was screaming 'I hate you', and then she screamed something about being beaten. What in the world is going on Dad? We're not kids anymore, hiding in our closets or under beds. Dad, again, we're here to ask you what's going on?" Ted asked, not really comfortable about confronting his dad, but after listening to Teresa's concern, it was time.

Charleton stood up and walked around the room then he spoke, "You too; it seems like everyone's on my case. I never beat your mother."

"Come on, Dad, we're not stupid. Today I talked with Frances. She told me some strange things. How come mom spent two weeks in her bedroom and we knew nothing about it. Why weren't we told it was something more serious than a cold? According to Frances it was definitely more than a cold. Why was there tape around her ribs? Come on Dad," Teresa said, confronting her dad with no holds barred.

"Frances is a good worker, but she talks too much," Charleton said, mumbling the last part of the sentence to himself as he looked out into the dark sky through the open vertical blinds. He saw some traffic moving in the distance and wished he could move with it, "Okay — okay! What is it you kids want me to say? Sometimes I'm a jerk. I do lose my temper. I'm not a perfect man, okay?"

"Dad, losing your temper is one thing but breaking someone's ribs is another. Tell us, was Frances right? You know we could talk to Doc Ellis; he'd tell us." Ted said getting up and walking over to his father who was growing more agitated by the moment, chewing on the ice in his glass and spitting it back into the glass, obviously irritated.

"Why, Dad, you know if mom pressed charges, you could have gone to jail and that was over a year ago. Why did you lie to us and say the reason mom was not up and walking around was because she had a cold. Why?" Teresa asked getting up also and walking toward his father.

"Okay, I stretched the truth some, but I didn't want to worry you two. I did lose my temper. I shoved her, but I didn't hit her, all right! I'm sorry, how many times must I say those words? Are you satisfied now? Sometimes she just pushes my buttons, and I blow up. Yeah, I yell a lot, but I never abused your mother. Now both of you get off my case!" Charleton said sharply with tears welling up in his eyes for some reason.

"Look dad, you say you're not a perfect man, but you expect all of us to be, especially mom. Nobody can be perfect. We're not here to pick on you, but enough is enough! Ted and I have both decided that if you ever hit mom again, call her stupid or mistreat her in any way, we will both disown you. We will no longer be a part of this family; you'll never see the grandkids again and we will help mom leave you. Families are supposed to be a sanctuary not a cemetery." Teresa said, unmoved by her father's anger and tears.

"Dad, I have always admired you, but I can no longer accept the way you treat our mother; she doesn't deserve that! She has as far as I know always been faithful to you. She's always been kind to you. She doesn't deserve to be treated the way you're treating her. She doesn't have to put up with your anger. Dad, we're not little kids like Teresa said, we don't have to run and hide anymore."

"It's time to change. No more beatings, no more harsh words, no more lies or as you say, stretching the truth. You might say you never beat mother, but we know better. Maybe that's our fault for sweeping things under the rug for so long, but enough is enough." Ted said firmly but tactfully as he put his hand on his father's shoulder, who cried as if he'd heard all these allegations for the very first time, but he knew he really hadn't. It's just coming from his flesh and blood. Their words seem to penetrate deeply into his soul.

Chapter 14

Carl Leonard, foreman of the Charleton's Road building division, had been a model worker until his divorce twelve months ago. It seemed after that, his whole world fell apart. His wife got the house, the boat, the luxury car and more than half the money. The only conciliation was that the kids were grown, so there was no fight over them.

Carl was hardened by time and his occasional binge drinking which at times had cost him his entire paycheck, which was creating a lot of problems for him. If liquor didn't take his paycheck, gambling did. He was always short on cash. He didn't attend church often but even that fell off until he just quit going all together.

He had arrived at the only place he could afford, a simple broken down one bedroom house just off old Route K by the Rockbridge Elementary School he had attended so many years ago as a child.

The house was in shambles with a leaky roof and loose shutters. It had old tile siding of black and pink, quite ugly really. The grass hadn't been cut in months, and the only other standing building was a metal shed, white and red, rusty and leaning to the right. It was late when Carl was about ready to go to bed. He was dressed in old white cut-off shorts and a dirty grey t-shirt when he saw a car's headlights shine in his bedroom window. He went to see who it was. As he parted the cheap yellow plastic curtains, he said to himself, "Not them again, I'm sick of those guys coming around here."

He closed the curtains and went to the back door; the floor creaked as he walked. He opened the door to see one short round guy with no hair and a tall guy with thickly braided hair. At first glance, they looked like the number 10 as they stood by each other. Both were dressed in grey suits with black ties.

"Hey Carl, old boy, the boss needs a few things" the short guy said with a wicked smile, causing his forehead to wrinkle.

"No, I can't! I did it before because I needed the money, but I won't do it anymore. My boss is too good to me. I can't keep stealing from him!" Carl pleaded. The taller of the men pulled out a straight razor from his jacket and held it to Carl's throat.

"Look pal, our boss Jonesy needs some stuff. When he needs stuff we get it for him, understand? He'll pay you well; he always does. Should I cut him Razzy?" the tall hoodlum asked, looking at his cohort, seeing him shake his head "no".

"No Sky, the boss didn't say kill him tonight. Here's the list. I got it in my pocket, it's simple," Razzy said, removing a creased list and putting it in front of Carl, after Sky withdrew the razor.

"Fine, I'll do it, just don't kill me." Carl said pleading for his life, then rubbing his throat, he mumbled aloud as he received the list from Razzy. "A five-thousand-gallon water tanker and a bulldozer! Don't you think this stuff will be missed? What are you trying to do, run Charleton out of business?"

"That's a fine idea Einstein." Razzy said, shaking his head at Carl's revelation.

"Okay, when and where? This is the last time I'm doing this; I really do need some big bucks. Buddy, if I get caught this time, I know it's jail time. I need some help moving the stuff." Carl said, shaking a little.

"Look, fine, we'll help. Don't worry, Jonesy will take good care of you, ff you take care of him, you understand?" Sky said, putting away his razor. He continued, "we want this stuff in forty-eight hours or else!"

"Or else, what?" Carl asked naively.

"Look, you came to us for ten grand, we gave it to you. We didn't come looking for you. You gave us some stuff in return. Just shut up, get the stuff and you won't have to find out about the 'or else'." Razzy said.

"Forty-eight hours, got it?" Sky said, shoving a 44-Magnum in Carl's face this time.

"I got it. Better yet, if you guys meet me at the Carrington Lane site the day after tomorrow, north of Canton, Missouri, Highway 61 North around 4:00 am, we can move the stuff then up to another site where we're not working yet, and it can't be seen from where we're at now. It rained yesterday, that's why I'm home today. It's a three-hour commute, but we'll working up there, I'm sure, by Thursday. Normally I stay up there during the week; but you guys know that already, I'm sure. You can load the stuff up later." Carl said knowing it was wrong but realizing he had no other choice.

"We'll be there; you'd better be up there too." Razzy said, withdrawing his gun.

They both turned and walked away after seeing Carl nod "no problem".

Carl shut the door. He was glad they were gone and wishing he'd never gotten involved with them. He's never met Jonesy personally, but he had heard he could be very ruthless, something he did not care to find out personally.

Chapter 15

As usual, Carl was the first one to arrive at work, it was still dark. The quietness of the early morning beauty, birds chirping and the morning sun glistening through the trees along the old roadway seemed to conflict with everything that was wrong with what he was doing. It was as if all Creation was going about life but watching him. He was busy, moving the equipment Jonesy had requested to a secluded part of the work area surrounded by trees, with the help of Jonesy's thugs. The only things he couldn't provide were the company pick-up trucks. Those are being driven by two senior employees that hadn't arrived yet.

When Carl arrived at the foreman's trailer, a little hurried, he noticed that Danner, the young man who was always eager to work, was already there and hanging around the trailer ready to punch in.

"Hey Carl, running a little late today, or am I a little early," Danner asked smiling, showing all his white teeth and eager to get to work.

"I'm a little late." Carl said looking at his watch and seeing it was 5:30 am. He always arrived at 5:00 am, never late. "Oh, wow that late! Well, you know once in a while us old men need a little extra sleep."

"Yeah, you're not getting any older buddy, you're getting better." Danner said, chuckling, causing his large frame to jiggle. "Hey Carl, I didn't think we were working up by route 'B' yet, you know that road that runs along the river. I came into work the back way this morning and noticed some of our equipment is there already."

Carl opened up the trailer door, realizing he may have been seen there or at the least his hiding place was known, "Oh yeah, the boss called, we need to start there tomorrow or wait, maybe this afternoon. Anyway, we need to start working down there soon. Don't worry son, it's all taken care of," Carl responded, trying not to act so nervous.

"Okay, as long as you got things under control. I won't worry about it. I guess I just like to know what's going on, that's all," Danner replied, not really questioning Carl any further. He had always seemed honest. He'd been working with him for the past year. Danner punched in and left the trailer as the others started arriving. He had his hard-hat on, grabbed his lunch, and he started up over the hill in back of the trailer toward the bulldozer. Something bothered him, he was sure they weren't going to be working on the Route "B" interchange for another month. At least that's what the big boss had let everyone know at a recent meeting to discuss how things were going. He knew Carl had been absent that day.

He waved to a few of his other employees. However, this continued to nag at him. Why was the equipment there? Eventually he shook it out of his mind and just did his work for the morning.

Carl remained back at the trailer office to get the coffee going and, as usual, he joked with the crew as they came and went, but he couldn't help but wonder if Danner had seen him earlier. He knew he hadn't said anything, but the wondering was bugging him anyway.

Around noon Danner arrived back at the trailer. Out of curiosity he had asked other employees about the Route 'B' interchange, and they all thought like he did. Especially Jack, a tall skinny man with a goatee, who operated a dump truck at the Carrington Lane site, he was saying the project wouldn't be started until late September. The situation bothered Danner to the point he and Jack got in Danner's '69 blue Camaro with headers and a high-rise manifold to go check it out. Carl watched them leave from the office window, but he wasn't sure just where they were headed.

"Hey Jack, be honest, is Carl acting a little strange to you?"

"Yep — ol' Crocket and I wanted to finish up laying gravel down for the bridge at the 'Culver Stockton get off' about two weeks ago, when we came back to punch out Carl was drinking from a brown paper bag. He never used to drink on the job," Jack said looking straight ahead, waving to his friends eating lunch on the road graders. On this ninety-five-degree day many were sitting in the shadow of their machine to stay a little cooler.

"Yeah, I heard his divorce was bad, he lost everything. Broke I guess he turned to the bottle. Charlotte and I will be married twenty-five years next month. If she ever left me, I'd probably do something stupid like that too. I know old man Magenta will fire you on the spot if he catches you drinking on the job. I have ten years here, I ain't taking that chance. What you said, yep, it was strange all that equipment was there at Route 'B', it doesn't make sense to me either."

"Yeah, I don't know. It seemed to be lined up like someone was gonna load it up," Danner said, driving closer to the area along some trees closer to the new road area which had been rooted up, but not yet cut up, so the big boys could come in and haul it away. The equipment seemed to be hidden behind the trees farthest from the highway. Danner looked in the same place and it was clean; there was nothing there.

"Hey Danner, I don't see nothing, are you sure this is the place?" Jack asked, dropping his jaw.

"I can't believe it!" Danner said stopping his car and getting out quickly, Jack followed. "The water tanker was over there, the bulldozer here, they've both disappeared!"

"And you came through at 5:00 am this morning?"

"Yes. Jack, I swear. I ain't lying to you." Danner said, walking in the tracks of the heavy equipment, trying to understand this mystery.

"Hey Danner, man, look over there, a low boy was here. Looks like somebody just loaded the stuff and took off. You said you didn't see anyone around?"

"No, it was all parked here like I said earlier. I asked Carl about it being over here and he told me that we were just going to start early. But the trees aren't gone yet, and the culvert pipe isn't here yet. What's going on Jack?" Danner asked, looking at Jack, whose long face and body made him look as straight as one of those trees that were standing along the highway.

"Maybe we got hit again. You know rumor has it there is a guy in town wanting to muscle in old man Magenta, maybe this is part of it."

"But why? Charleton Magenta is the best boss I ever had. Though I've never really talked to him face to face, he pays us well, gives us a lot of vacation time and lets us off for emergencies! Why is he the target?" Danner asked, waving his hand in the air not knowing what the answer could be.

"Who knows man, the good guys in this world always seem to come out on the short end of the stick. Let's go talk to Carl, he ought to be told." Jack said heading for the car. Danner went too and they drove quickly back to the trailer where Carl was eating a simple lunch of bologna and American cheese, with runny mustard oozing from the sides.

"Carl! Carl! Somebody got us and got us good!" both Danner and Jack said excitedly entering the trailer.

"Wait, slow down, what are you guys talking about?" Carl asked while putting his sandwich down on wax paper.

"Carl, it's about all the equipment that's gone from Route 'B'." Danner said, still breathless.

"What? It's gone! We're supposed to be working up there soon. How can that be?" Carl asked, trying to act surprised.

"It's gone! Like it vanished! We just saw some low boy tracks, someone stole it. We'd better call the police!" Jack said excitedly, seemingly liking this kind of adventure.

"Gone? I can't believe it! It must be those guys that have been stealing from us the last few months. Fellas go back to work. I'll call the police and Charleton. I'll take care of everything." Carl said, trying to look shocked. He stood up and headed them both toward the door patting them on the back. Then he continued, "Thanks for letting me know I'll call the cops right now. You just go back to work. I'm sure the police will get the low life scum who's steeling from us."

Danner and Jack went back to their jobs, but for some reason Danner didn't believe Carl. He sounded too calm and collected. Danner felt there was something much deeper at stake here and he was determined to find out what it was.

Chapter 16

The General sat quietly in his large home office with wood paneling and newspapers from the New York Times to the Times of London. He was trying to calculate the damage to Charleton's campaign. The negative publicity was so bad due to his wife's tirade that one of the Large News Outlets had plastered Charleton's picture on the front page, headlined above the caption, "Would you want a wife beater for Governor?" With his coffee cup, large and full, he was making notes on a yellow legal pad when Charleton entered, a little tired but seemed level headed. "Hello Charlie, have a seat," the General said pointing to a blue cushioned chair with no arms. Charleton sat down staring at a huge portrait of Winston Churchill, the one that Yousuf Karsh had snapped just after he had snatched a cigar out of Churchill's mouth, which many say helped galvanize the British war efforts.

"Boy, every time I see Churchill's portrait I want to go to war."

"Well, you may have to. Do you realize that since that episode at your home, Charlie, one of the news organizations said if the Governor's race would be held today, you'd get less than two percent of the vote, which I assume would be family and friends, if you have any left!"

"Do you realize your wife's rantings may have destroyed your chances? Our chances? I thought you said you talked it over with her. According to eyewitnesses that wasn't the case. You lied to me Charlie. You told me a bold face lie." The General scolded, pointing his bony index finger at Charleton.

"Sorry, I guess I assumed it would be all right. I didn't mean to lie! I mean she usually goes along with whatever I choose anyway," Charleton said reluctantly, feeling like a school kid that just got caught lying.

"If you want me to help you, you have got to be truthful with me 100% of the time. Answer me; did you ever strike your wife? Do you realize that tonight on Larry King, Kelly Farber is going to be on the show? I do hope you recognize the name," the General said, staring at Charleton, who started to flinch, wishing he had not come.

"Kelly Farber, yes, I remember her, a very good domestic — but she was a little too nosey, even after she signed the gag order on what went on at Southwood Hills. She still ran her mouth. Why, there were rumors floating around that she signed a book deal to tell all. I just can't believe that woman. I gave her a job — she stayed in our home. She got paid time off and she's stabbing us in the back. What an ungrateful …. Well, I had to fire her six months ago and …" Charleton said with disgust and mumbling some other words to himself as the General interrupted him like people do when they have something more important to say.

"Do you have any idea what she's going to talk about tonight? The only reason I found out early is the fact I have connections. She's gonna swear that you beat your wife, that you actually broke her ribs once and you tried to hide the fact by keeping her locked in the bedroom for 2 weeks! How do you think NOW will take this, or the National Council on Child Abuse & Family Violence? Your name is mud right now. Tell me, did you ever strike your wife? Be straight with me Charlie. Don't beat around the bush," the General asked, looking Charleton right in the eye. Before he answered he got up and walked around.

"General, we've had our fights over the years like most couples do, but I've always treated her good. If I hit her, do you think she'd stay with me for over thirty years?" Charleton asked as he walked slowly back to the General, who scratched his bald head moving his stocking cap around.

"No but, I can guarantee you one thing, Charlie, if you're lying to me with all the digging going on around now in your life and your family's life somebody's gonna find out something. I hope there are no more skeletons in your closet. No out of wed-lock kids or anything else that could scandalize you?"

"No, not that I know of anyway. Look, General, I honestly don't know why my wife acted that way, but it won't happen again."

"I do want to be the next Governor. I think I could help this state." Charleton said proudly — walking back toward the General.

"Okay, I believe you Charlie, but I'll level with you, I'll be watching your life too, and if I find out you lied to me again, I'll drop my support so fast it will make your head swim! Got it Charlie?"

"Got it sir! Got it!"

"Great. Look, I've written your speech for next Friday to make your official announcement to the press about the fiasco at your home and hopefully it will revive your entry into the 2004 election. Lay low for now, avoid the press. I know they're like bad food sometimes — they're everywhere. And learn that speech! If we pull together and work hard, we might be able to pull this off, we just might," the General said, pulling out a white folder from under his yellow legal pad — he continued, "learn this; your political life may depend on it."

After leaving the General's office, Charleton got back into his limo, lit up a Davidoff cigar — his favorite — poured himself a swig of Macallan Scotch. He asked Joe to drive him around to some of his project sites although he really didn't want to see any of them. He just needed time to think about his wife and their relationship. He thought about how bad things had gotten and he reasoned to himself "I'm a real Jerk! I give her everything. I mean she can walk into any store and buy anything. Absolutely nothing is out of reach for her. She really ought to be happy."

He mused awhile then he started to mumble to himself, "happiness, what does that mean? My wife — maybe she needs to just grow up! Yes, yes, she does like to argue. Me too. I suppose that's just my boss side coming out of me. But I shouldn't argue at all with the one I love. I remember when we had nothing, when I had to practically beg for work. I came home and we loved on each other all night — now, nothing."

Charleton paused for a moment as he felt the limo stop at a red light. He said to Joe, his driver, "take me to Paris Road, those townhomes we're building there, I need to check on them."

"Fine sir. May I ask, are you all right? You just seem a little irritated," Joe said, glancing in his rearview mirror at his boss who was basically ignoring him for a few seconds and then responded, "Just drive there, just drive."

Joe did just that; but, being a devout man, he prayed silently for Charleton and about everything that was happening to him. He also, like so many others, hated the way he treated his wife, and he wondered within himself why he didn't intervene more. Joe silently continued to drive. Charleton mumbled again to himself and seemed a little irritated. "What does Joe know? A little irritated? Not hardly. I'm a lot irritated! Constance, my own wife, will hardly say anything to me. I walk in my family room, and she walks out. We dine together and all I can hear is knives, forks and spoons. I just can't take the silent treatment anymore. I'm ready to explode and my own kids think I have abused my own wife, their mother. Why, they're crazy too! The whole world is crazy! The guy from Fredly's Windows just shook his head at me when he replaced the picture window, like I caused my wife to jump through the window. Come on, how can I cause that? Yes, we yell too much.

Yes, sometimes I probably cross the line. She just needs to listen to me more often. I really do love her! I really do! What is going on? She's just avoiding me now! She doesn't even kiss me anymore unless you count air kisses. Making love has gone out the window. I just can't take this silent treatment anymore. I just can't!"

"Sir."

"Yes, what is it, Joe?"

"We're here," Joe said, stopping in front of a large construction site full of bulldozers, cement trucks and lots of workers with hardhats, all with a big M on the front.

"Okay. Okay." Charleton said as he started to get out. He finished his liquor, put his cigar out, shook his head and mumbled once more, "Something's gotta change or I'm gonna lose it. Something just has to!"

Chapter 17

Constance who had mostly tried to avoid everyone, was awed by all the flowers and cards sent during her convalescence. She was ready to achieve some normalcy of life after being cooped up in her room for the last ten days.

The scars on her face were not so severe that a little heavier than usual make-up could hide them. As for her scars, one just beneath her eye for some reason when she had first seen it, she continued to stare at it. She wondered what had caused it to take such an odd healing pattern. At first, she had tried to cover it up, but she was angered because she had always hated scars. Somehow the scar prompted her to reflect on that horrible night her mother died. However, the longer she looked in her vanity mirror the more she realized it wasn't a bad scar — it actually looked like, yes, like a small rose, a delicate freshly bloomed rose. She began to wonder to herself if God had caused the scar to heal that way to remind her, she was still valuable and she was still worth something in this life. As for the scars on her arms and legs, those could be easily hidden by her style of clothing.

Constance was sad that Teresa had flown back to her family in Australia, though she had begged her to stay a few more days. But she made a promise of a longer holiday visit in November, she accepted her departure. With Teresa gone, her message of no longer putting up with Charleton's abuse still lingered; she did think seriously about leaving him for good. She was finally tired of the beatings, both emotional, and physical.

Constance today had decided to finally visit Tonya and Pookie after a few back-and-forth phone calls on her personal cell phone. She was ready for some sunshine.

After taking a long, slow, hot bath in her Venetian designed master bathroom of white and yellow — trimmed in gold with an eight-foot Jacuzzi, square with large maidens holding white and gold candles on their heads. All in front of three curved block windows with an etched white frame mirror at the foot of a huge tub. She let the bubbles and suds soothe her problems away and for some reason during that bath time she began to think about her childhood, she realized it hadn't been all bad. Her dad hadn't always been a maniac. He had on occasion been very kind to her, taking time to read to her. Her favorite book had been L. Frank Baum's *The Wonderful Wizard of Oz*. Oh, she knew she had identified with Dorothy, and she just wanted to go "over the rainbow", especially loving the Emerald City with its horses of a different color. Sometimes she wished she could change just as quickly to be someone other than herself; but then again, when her dad and mom took to the park near their home where they both played with her on the swings, on the merry-go-round and teeter-totter, she felt special.

She remembered there seemed to be love, lots of love until she became five. That's when her dad got fired from the University where he taught English. How could he have an affair with the Dean's seventeen-year-old daughter? She was an accelerated student in his class. Of course, her father denied it, but her mother found the girl's clothing in their car, he still denied it. Their marriage was never the same; trust had been broken.

Her father never got a better job. He started drinking and her parents started fighting until there was no more love left. Constance always thought about why her mother stayed in the relationship with her father, and through the years she realized that it was because her mother loved her more than anything in the whole world. She had heard later through her aunt Josephine, who raised her until she was ten, that her mother had a bad bicycle accident riding a boy's bike, and because of that she was never supposed to be able to have children, but she had one little girl, her.

Constance loved her Aunt Josephine. She had three kids, all older than she was, and a husband who thought the world of all of them. They all went to church, loved God and held hands at meals, at home or a restaurant to pray for the food. They never seemed embarrassed about their God. Aunt Josephine died of cancer and her husband shortly after in an automobile crash, many said he died from a broken heart. All the children were put into foster care, including her.

Constance, who from age eight on, never saw her father again. He had been convicted and judged insane and sent to the State Mental Hospital supposedly for life or until he was deemed no longer a danger to society. She had decided she wanted no further contact with him after he murdered her mother. Religion to her seemed vague, and unsure, an unknowable thing, that's why she always questioned God "on why didn't He stop her father from doing that to her mother if He was indeed a loving God?"

She never did understand this, but she did finally go the religious route — when she was about fifteen, she professed Christ, but forgiving others for the wrong they did to her still troubled her. She never did get the concept of forgiveness, instead she still harbored resentment for her father, who did try and reach out to her through the mail when she became a successful socialite and was in the media from time to time for charitable causes. She returned the letters unopened.

Constance did think a lot about God, that it had to be Him allowing her to be so wealthy, allowing her to never want for food like she often did as a child, except while with Aunt Josephine. Or now, never again having to sleep in a cold apartment where rats roamed around like snoopy tenants. She felt grateful for her life, but so many days she just didn't feel happy.

She wanted to feel as happy as she did when her mom and dad would push her on the swing, and she would stretch her toes as far as she could to maybe touch a passing cloud.

After this last episode, Constance really avoided her husband. She didn't know how to deal with him. She had now seen all the news reports; she'd seen all the shows commenting on her emotional fitness. She didn't feel like she was crazy, instead she just wanted to be loved, feel loved and appreciated, all of which she felt her husband didn't care about.

After reading Tonya's letter a few times, Constance began to wonder if Tonya and Pookie would welcome her into their life. She had always liked Tonya, who seemed simple and kind, but her downfall was that she wasn't quite as refined and elegant as she was; this caused an occasional clash but never to the point that hurtful remarks were made.

So, after bathing and putting on a soft skirt, light blue blouse, stockings and heels, she left the estate, only telling others she was going out for a drive.

Behind the wheel she felt alive for the first time in months. She was usually chauffeured, but this time she drove her new Maserati Spyder her husband had given her on her last birthday. She drove south of the freeway toward the airport, then she took a country road west that led to a park which was quiet. It had a few older picnic tables, green refuse containers, mostly full, as if they hadn't been emptied for months and a small concrete toilet with separate sides for men and women — painted blue on one side and pink on the other. The park had a small rainbow-colored merry-go-round, two green teeter-totters and swings with black seats and rusty chains. There were tall trees, an old badminton net and an old sand volleyball pit. Just to the south of the parking area was a cave for exploring with a shallow brook running through it. Most of the park's visitors, which weren't many, went there.

Constance drove up to see a young woman about 20 chasing a little boy about two around a picnic table. The girl grabbed the child and smashed her face into his stomach causing him to laugh hysterically. She knew immediately that it was Tonya and Pookie. She waved as she got out and locked her car. They ran toward her after seeing her walk stiffly toward them.

"Hi Mrs. Magenta, I'm glad you could come, it's been a while," Tonya smiled and said, telling Pookie to say hi grandma. Pookie looked at the strange woman smelling her perfume; he lifted his little hand to give her a high five which Constance did laughing a little, "Boy he's a cutie. Tonya, it's good to see you. It's been much too long," Constance said leaning toward them, hugging them together.

"I'm so glad you came. When you didn't write or call, I thought you might not want to meet, but it was nice to hear from you the other day. Are you feeling ok?" Tonya asked, being sensitive having seen and heard the news reports. She put Pookie down — he immediately headed for the merry-go-round; both women followed him.

"I had some personal things to deal with, yes, I'm ok. Now Pookie, you be careful," Constance said watching her grandson climb the merry-go-round, "hold on tight."

"He will, the problem is getting him off. He always throws a fit, but he's a good boy. You really look so nice today." Tonya said softly, sensing a little unhappiness in Constance.

"Thank you. You know Teresa, my daughter came for a visit — she lives in Australia with her Pastor husband — I believe you met her once — they have twin girls that are almost two."

"That's great! She always did have a level head on her shoulders. Now, hold on. Momma will push you harder — here I go — wheeee," Tonya said momentarily running along the dirt path left by other parents along the side of the merry-go-round.

"You look great too and you look so happy. Please call me Constance; Mrs. Magenta is much too formal. Are you still in school?" Constance asked, waving at Pookie as he went round and round, she realized he did indeed look like her son, Ted.

"Yes, I'm going to get a master's degree in child psychology from Stephen's College. I would like to counsel children, especially those who had a real hard start in life, I figure if someone could straighten them out before their teens, maybe they would become contributors to society instead of just takers," Tonya said letting the merry-go-round slow down, much to the dismay of Pookie.

"Go- Mommy. Go." Pookie said, bouncing around on the metal floor of the merry-go-round with his little bottom.

"Swing, go swing," Tonya said heading towards the swings. She watched her son continue to make a fuss — finally realizing his tantrum wasn't going to work, he got off the merry-go-round and headed for the swing where his mother helped him up and she pushed him.

"I did appreciate your letter and talking to you over the phone and I do desire a relationship with you and Pookie. You both seem so happy."

"Great Mrs. M, I mean Constance, like I said in my letter, I'm not the same girl I was; Jesus gave me hope! He gave me life, and He gave me a son!"

"Dad convinced me that all of you need to be a part of Pookie's life. Constance, I know Ted may or may not want to be, but that shouldn't stop you or your husband or Teresa. I believe, Constance, that a family is what is most important. It's not about the cars, homes or clothes. I'm not talking about you, but rather people in general. Maybe I can't give Pookie everything. My father, you know, the Reverend Green, is well off, but not quite like you. You know we didn't have much growing up, but I did know one thing and that was: my father loved me when I did wrong, and he loved me when I did right. He loved me."

"My father used to say that when I lay my head down on my pillow at night I should never ever have to wonder if he loved me or not, well, with mom it was a different story."

"It's love Constance; it's unconditional love that makes the world go round."

"Yes, Pookie gets into things. He messes up the house leaving his toys out all over the place, but when it's all said and done, he's my son and nothing or no one can ever change that," Tonya said proudly — pushing her son higher into the air. Constance watched him scream, "Wheee," she momentarily closed her eyes remembering when her parents used to do the same thing with her and how happy she felt. She was so lost in her reflection that she didn't realize the strange man who had parked near her car was taking photos of all three of them while sitting in his vehicle, an old red van.

CHAPTER 18

It was a rather tranquil, but late dinner that Constance and Charleton had in the informal dining room just off the kitchen, sitting at the cherry table set with flowers and candles. The dialed back chandelier and eight lights dripping with crystal cast a rather eerie glow on a large original painting of a fox hunt, perfectly hung above a highly polished gold tea set and centered on the large matching cherry buffet. For some reason when Constance stared at the painting with the men dressed in knickerbockers and riding handsome horses with hounds at their feet, her eyes became focused on the red fox who seemed terrified, as if the fox knew that had met its end. She finally turned away as her husband sat across from her wearing a hand-sewn suit minus the jacket. He had briefly smiled at her, and she smiled back quickly, but not without her sensing the phoniness of the moment. Her mind still wandered back to the park with Tonya and Pookie. She could still see the happiness, the swings and the merry-go-round. She could still feel the warm air on her face, but all that was wiped away by the thoughts of whether she should tell Charleton or not about his grandson. Constance pursed her lips and decided not to say anything for now. At least for the moment, they weren't at war with each other. The atmosphere currently was a bit cozier than intended.

The table was set with various baked breads, crescent rolls, sweet butters, pistos and fideos with mussels, clams and salsa verde with a dessert of Turkish coffee, ice cream with cardamom on casual china trimmed in gold with monogrammed goblets.

The only interruption in their meal together was by Frances who wanted them to finish so she could clean up. She had also complimented Mrs. M on her soft yellow lounge pantsuit.

It was now 7:30 pm.

"How was your day, Dear?" Charleton asked softly, as if not to speak too loudly and, as if he knew just one word or tone might set her off again into another tirade. Ever since she had gotten home from the hospital, he was walking on eggshells with her. So as not to cause any uneasiness in her, he had chosen to call her Dear instead of Babe. He knew she became infuriated whenever he called her Babe, and they weren't really getting along at all now.

"Fine. How was your day?" Constance returned respectfully. As soon as she watched her husband cutting up his food with a marble-handled knife, a bad memory shot through her, but she kept her composure.

They both remained silent for a few more minutes, as if they really were just trying to think of what to say next. It had been this way for the last few weeks, which really bothered Charleton. Finally, he was tired of just hearing forks, spoons and knives and swallowing. He spoke loudly by just slamming his fist hard on the table, causing the goblets and silverware to jump up from the table clinking and clanking. "Enough already! Enough! Why won't you talk to me, other than small talk? Geez, you act like I have AIDS or something worse!"

Constance, who was more shaken by his outburst, was frightened at first. She tried to control herself as she remembered something her daughter had told her before she left — "the one who angers you is the person who controls you …" So, with that she thought, she'd just respond to her irritated husband, "Maybe I just don't want to talk to you right now."

"Well, I do want you to talk to me!" Charleton blurted back.

Constance, not wanting to get into a confrontation, realized she really needed to speak up and a boldness rose up inside her that startled her. Despite the growing tension she remained composed, "That's the problem, the whole problem with us right now. It's always what you want to do. Did it ever occur to you that I may not want to be a Governor's wife? Did you even think to ask me? Yes, I've listened to CNN, Bill Moyer, Larry King and all the others. Everyone thinks I'm crazy, but I'm not! I guess if I'm anything right now I'm just tired. I'm tired of life, I'm tired of being treated as second class by you, and I am really tired of you if you want to know the truth. I'm not trying to hurt your feelings, Charleton, but I can't live with you anymore. I really need to be gone from here. I just can't do it anymore." Constance spoke slowly and distinctly, as if she'd waited to say these words for a long time.

"What are you saying? You want to leave me? No, you can't! Why?" Charleton said. Dropping his fork, he got up and went over to her side of the table and reached out to her.

"Don't touch me! Don't you ever touch me again! Charleton, I don't love you anymore," Constance said, seeing Charleton grow more agitated. She hurriedly got up and started to turn away, which infuriated Charleton so much that he grabbed her from behind and spun her around. She kicked and wiggled furiously and shouted, "Let me go! Don't touch me!"

"Listen woman, no one walks away from me; you are my wife. Sit your butt down, and let's talk this thing out," Charleton blurted while furiously trying to force her back into her chair.

"No! Let me go! Now! Frances, help! Help!" Constance said kicking and screaming, hitting the table with her body, causing filled glasses to fall over, soiling the white tablecloth trimmed in gold. Frances came in quickly to find Constance in her husband's grip.

"Mr. M! Let her go! What are you doing? Let her go or I'll call the police!" Frances said, her mouth open, seeing this struggle.

Charleton immediately let go as he saw Frances enter, "Oh-no, it's not what you think, ha' we were just blowing off a little steam that's all." Charleton said letting his wife go and trying to straighten her clothes for her.

However, as soon as she was free, she ran out of the dining room, bursting into tears. Frances looked at Charleton in utter disdain and ran to comfort Constance.

Charleton yelled loud enough so that everyone could hear, "Aargh! What in the world am I doing?" he plopped down in his chair, sighed, trying to regain his composure. He rubbed his face in his hands realizing he had just done a very stupid thing and right now he felt he had no way to correct it. Tears came over him out of nowhere.

Constance ran into the family room and threw herself across a beige overstuffed sofa; her shoulders were heaving heavily. Frances dropped to the floor beside her head and hugged her doing her best to console her.

"Mrs. M., It'll be alright. There, there," Frances said, almost treating her like a child.

"He hates me so much; my own husband hates me! Why does he hate me so much?" Constance asked, her words muffled by her arms smashing into her face.

"He should have never touched you, blowing off steam, no way! Should I call the police? He assaulted you," Frances said seriously, realizing that she'd seen this type of behavior, which could lead to something worse.

"No, I have to get out — I have got to leave. I can't take this anymore. I'm scared! I'm really scared!" Constance mumbled. She was shaking as she sat up a little to see Frances who was still angry at Mr. M.

"Yes, he treats you so badly. You must do something now! Mrs. M.; you must!"

"Yes, but I … I'm" Constance said — stuttering, bursting into more tears as she heard the door chimes echo, seemingly through the whole house.

Both she and Frances heard an, "I'll get it," from the kitchen — they let him get it.

Charleton walked slowly to the door, his hair disheveled after running his fingers through it, wondering how to make it up to Constance. His eyes red from crying after hearing her cries filter down the hallway, he was even more confused about why he had been so stupid — to make his wife cry and hate him so.

"Hi Danner, what brings you here this late?"

"Sir, sorry to come by your home, are you all right? If I may say so, you look a little stressed," Danner returned after seeing his boss's haggard look.

"Long day, come in. what brings you here at this hour of the night?" Charleton asked softly, slowly getting his composure back as he let the young man in who was a little excited about something.

"Thanks, I really didn't mean to disturb you, but I tried to reach you at your office and when I couldn't I tried here at your home, but whoever answered the phone said to expect you around that time. Sir, did Carl call you today?" Danner asked, standing in the huge vestibule — admiring the lavish furnishings, especially the one-hundred-and-fifty-year-old Serapi rug in the vestibule.

"No, why, was he supposed to?" Charleton asked, looking quite puzzled.

"Ah — is that someone crying, sir?" Danner said, turning his head toward the family room where the sound was coming from.

"Ignore that, son, about Carl — what about him?"

"Carl, oh, he didn't call you or the police?" Danner asked, still bugged about the crying.

"No, no police — spit it out."

"Okay, just as I thought. See Sir, when I went to work today, I stayed with a sick friend last night so, I came to work the back way out by the Route B intersection, and I saw a bunch of our equipment there. I asked Carl and he said you had moved the starting date sooner rather than later for grading the Carrington Lane site, but I asked around and everyone said that wasn't to start until late September. Anyway, something sounded fishy, so Jack and I checked it out at lunch and all the equipment was gone, a five-thousand-gallon water tanker and a dump truck. Jack and I checked it out and we saw low-boy tracks. Well, when we saw this, we drove back to talk to Carl — he said not to worry — that he'd phone you and the police …" Danner said seeing his boss get angry and shaking his head, interrupting him.

"Carl? Not Carl, why would he do this to me? I can't believe it. He's been my best foreman for years. Maybe I need to pay him a visit soon, like maybe tonight!" Charleton said, shaking his head.

"Sir, I'm so sorry to say this, but I'm around him every day and he's been awfully irritated over the littlest things. I know where he lives, if you want, I can take you there. I'd like to talk to him too. He's been like a father to me. We can take my car if you don't mind." Danner said heading for the door.

Charleton yelled down the hall, "I'll be back later," basically to anyone who cared to listen.

Charleton shut the door behind him and went toward Danner's restored '67 Camaro — it looked great! It almost looked black in the lamp lights and footlights along the main entryway.

As they drove along, Charleton kept mumbling, "Carl, I can't believe, Carl?"

Danner heard this and responded, "Sir, it's a shock to me too, but again I hate to bring up more bad news, but Jack Tonie said he worked one night and caught Carl drinking on the job."

"Divorce, divorce can destroy a man. It seemed like it did Carl, boy oh boy. Hey Danner, you ever been married son? I guess if I don't change the subject a little, I'm gonna be so mad when I see Carl, I'll probably tear him limb from limb because nobody steals from Charleton Magenta, nobody!" Charleton said looking out the window and trying to wish this night away. First, a fight with his wife, then finding out his foreman is stealing from him!"

"Well sir, almost. I thought I was dating the right girl anyway. I mean I was a senior in High School when I met Liz — Liz Burton.

My, she was gorgeous. I transferred from Moberly to Rock Bridge Senior High. It was just my mother and me. Well, I played football. I guess I was pretty good — I made All-State tight end. Well, Liz was, I thought, the perfect girl, smart, gorgeous and real lady. We dated for a while, and I thought she was the one. I know this is gonna sound crazy, but after the first month all she wanted to do was sleep with me. I was raised better than that. Like I said it was just my mother and me, my dad died in Viet Nam, so my mother did her best to guide me by the Bible. I became a Christian at ten years of age, and it was drilled into me you only go to bed with your wife."

"Well, Liz came on to me so strongly that I finally told her women are better than the way she was acting. My mother told me most women are going to be treated like a tool or a treasure.... A tool is tossed aside in an old toolbox under rusty nuts and bolts and screwdrivers while a treasure is something that needs to be shined up and displayed to the world, something never to be ashamed of, so I broke it off because I wanted a woman who wanted to be treated like a treasure, someone who wanted to be cherished. I guess I haven't found her yet."

Charleton sat quietly soaking in what the young man had just said. It dawned on him, he hadn't been treating Constance like a treasure at all but like a tool, yes, he knew that was the case.

"Sir, are you all, right? I hope I'm not boring you. You're mighty quiet." Danner said genuinely concerned for his boss.

"Just thinking, oh I hope you find your treasure, your lady someday. What was stolen, tell me again?"

"A water tanker and one dump-truck."

"Man, 'o man, the insurance company will love to hear about this. Carl lives here? What a dump! His house needs to be condemned." Charleton said, noticing the ragged looking property. The grass was so high you could barely see a rusty lawn mower hiding under the only weak yellow porch light.

Danner stopped the car. They both got out and walked toward the house, only a small light in the bedroom was on.

Charleton arrived first at the door and knocked. Both of them could see through the diamond shaped window in the door. Lights were coming on as Carl in a t-shirt and short pants moved groggily toward the door, finally opening it.

"Charleton, ah, Danner, you guys are out kinda late. What do you need?" Carl asked, cracking the door a bit, speculating why they had come.

"Carl, let us in. You and I need to talk now!" Charleton exclaimed forcefully.

"Okay," Carl said, opening the door that led to the kitchen where so many dishes were piled up with half eaten meals and roaches scattering everywhere when the lights came on. Beer cans and liquor bottles were everywhere; so many that they looked like a Modernist sculpture.

"Carl, why, why did you steal from me — from my company? I know you were told about the theft this afternoon. You were supposed to call me and the police, but you didn't because if you did the police would have notified me, why Carl?" Charleton asked, getting right in Carl's face as he backed against the filthy counter with half eaten cans of Pork and Beans with spoons still in them and roaches feasting on the contents.

"Who told you I was involved? Danner? Did you open your big mouth?" Carl asked while pointing at Danner.

"I just asked you to call the police. When I heard nothing on the radio or the news, not to mention the way you acted about the Route B project, I put two and two together. I'm sorry Carl, the boss needed to know." Danner said, not at all feeling afraid of Carl; rather he was feeling sorry for him. It was difficult to see someone he admired go so wrong.

Carl looked at Danner then at Charleton and sat down on his one and only vinyl and chrome kitchen chair and started to cry. He confessed through his tears, "I'm sorry Charleton. I'm sorry I spoke to you that way Danner. I don't know what got into me. I don't know. Ever since Charlotte left my whole world fell apart. I didn't have a home; I didn't have a wife. I started drinking more, sometimes drinking my take home pay. I couldn't make rent so with what money I could pull together I tried the Lottery, then gambling boats. I got so broke that a friend turned me on to Jonesy and…."

"Wait, not Jonesy, the hoodlum, he's nothing but scum! Don't tell me you borrowed money from that loan shark?" Charleton asked, cutting Carl off, realizing his story was getting worse.

"Yeah, he lent me ten grand and all I had to do was set up equipment so he could get his hands on it. Sorry, it was me," Carl said blubbering badly.

"Oh, what a mess — Jonesy came to me a few months back wanting me to be partners with him or else. He never told me what the 'or else' was, but I don't run from thugs like him. I quit running a long time ago." Charlton said boldly as he walked over and put his large hand on Carl's shoulder.

"I'm sorry, I'm really sorry Charleton."

"I believe you are, but I can't just sweep this situation under the rug. I guess I just don't understand, if you needed money, how come you didn't just come to me?"

"I don't know, I really don't know," Carl said, shaking his head, crying, his eyes red.

"Look, you go to work tomorrow as usual, get the crew going then come see me. I'll phone the police. Come see me, we'll work something out." Charleton said, pursing his lips and leaning his head toward the door, "Carl, lay off the booze. I'll trust you'll be in my office no later than 9:00 am. Danner, let's go. Carl, I'm disappointed in you, yes, I thought about tearing you limb from limb. Call it crazy but I don't change friends like some people change socks. I'm still your friend."

"Me too," Danner quipped, seeing Charleton's compassion.

Carl looked up through cloudy eyes and tried to smile, knowing indeed he had one friend left in this world, maybe two.

༄༅།

Constance, with Frances' help, made it to her bed. Somehow the large four poster bed with silk sheets was comfortable most nights, but tonight the bed seemed cold and stiff like she was sleeping on a burlap sack, like she had on occasion done as a young girl. It seemed her tears never stopped, she still wanted to leave, but something was telling her to stay.

As she pulled the covers up, waiting for her husband to come home, she had no idea where he went, and she realized for perhaps the first time, he could really kill her. She reflected on her broken ribs, which he declared was just an accident, when he had just wanted her to shut up about his late nights at the office. She had accused him of sleeping around and he pushed her into the bathroom. She slipped on the wet tile floor, landing on the edge of the huge ball and claw bathtub in the spare bathroom while the Venetian master bathroom was being installed. Accident, perhaps, she tried to reason. It was shortly after her recovery that she was off to the Sanderson Hotel in London on their private jet for two weeks. What about the time he slapped her so hard across the face during a surprise bash just for him and the kids that she had a hair line fracture — all because the steak she cooked for him, when Frances was off, was cooked medium/well instead of medium/rare. Constance remembered after she had recovered, he had taken her to an antique auction in New York. There she purchased an original Louis XV silhouette with a sunny palette of khaki, soft coral and gentle green and an original Balmoral secretary desk.

Constance knew after all the fights, Charleton always made up somehow. He always said he was sorry, and it seemed so, because she knew it could be 2, 3 or even 6 months before he yelled at her again or touched her improperly. Somehow things seem different this time. She knew that a gift or a trip wasn't going to smooth things over this time. She was feeling hurt both on the inside and the outside at the same time. The only thing she could think of was leaving. She just had to get away. After all, she didn't want to end up like her mother.

With that thought she shivered as she heard the front door open. She could hear someone coming up the stairs and slowly, deliberately turn the knob to the bedroom, which was dark. She felt afraid.

Constance was lying on her side when the door opened to reveal the outline of her husband. She couldn't see his face to see whether he was still mad or not. She heard him stop at the long heavy dresser and unload his pockets. Then without a word he went into the bathroom. She heard him undress, brush his teeth, gargle and take a quick shower. Constance heard his footsteps coming and a drawer near her open. She could see his silhouette putting on his pajamas. He quietly got into bed not saying a word, but she felt his rear-end touch hers, which was a sign he was still angry with her. When everything was alright between them, he always turned her toward him.

Constance pretended to be asleep as she heard her husband finally drift off, snoring as usual. She tried desperately to sleep but one part of her wanted to get up and fly away. The other part wanted to stay and try one more time. It seemed to her those two options were going back and forth like a ping-pong game that had gone on for much, much too long.

Chapter 19

Charleton left the estate before Constance had awakened. His sleep under the circumstances was acceptable, six hours. He dressed quickly and tried to arrange the day's activities, his wife, as usual, was not one of them. He still hadn't decided what to do about her. He knew he had to do something really spectacular to appease her this time. He just didn't know what. However, today his real concern seemed to be how to handle Carl. He had been with Charleton since his deck building days before the company exploded into the Fortune 500 Company that it was now. Carl also owned a farm, so he had only worked part-time for Charleton. When the farm crisis came in the 1980s, he lost it and went to work for Charleton full-time.

Carl, Charleton knew had always been on time. He and his crew were always under budget and always swept and garnished the project through the last day of work.

Charleton had noticed that recently he had missed a few more days in the last year, but he just chalked it up to Carl's age, nothing more. He knew they were good friends, yes, they drank a little together, they bowled a little together and once they were even partners in a three-legged race at a company picnic held each July. They won the race which made all of this really hard to understand.

As Charleton was headed to his office he rolled his window down for some fresh air and saw Jonesy's black limo parked beside a small pawn shop and check cashing store on West Broadway. There were two thugs standing alongside the car as if they were waiting for someone to come out of the shop.

Charleton knew that Jonesy was not a good person to be around day or night. Everyone in town knew he was involved in gambling out on the East coast and he had recently moved to the Midwest to get his hooks in gambling, procuring, massage parlors, and show girl clubs, plus the meth scene.

The problem, Charleton knew, was Jonesy would take his money, wrap it up into so many legitimate businesses and then transfer the funds to offshore islands where the US couldn't touch it. He was a brilliant but dishonest businessman which made it hard for the authorities to charge him with any crime.

Rumor had it Jonesy had been brought up on the RICO status, but mysteriously the witnesses against him disappeared and were never heard from again.

The DA kept coming after him, trying to get to him through his wife, who was tired of finding him with girls young enough to still be in junior high. Unfortunately, she was found hanging from a meat hook in a deserted beef processing warehouse, but Charleton never backed down from a threat.

Yes, he had phoned the police, but he knew the bureaucrats would not devote a lot of time to the investigation because commercial theft was surely not a priority.

Charleton motioned for Joe, his driver, to pull over beside Jonesy's limo. "Wait here," he said.

Charleton got out and walked to the back window, street side and it wasn't a second later that he had guns pointed in both his sides of his ribs by two thugs.

"Pal, what are you doing? Get your hands off the car," the tall thug said.

"Back off, I just wanted to talk to your boss for a minute," Charleton said, not acting scared at all. "What's all the commotion?" A voice was heard from inside the car, the tinted window slowly rolled down to reveal an old man wearing a wide tie with a large diamond tie clip that matched his diamond cufflinks trimmed in gold and a double-barreled shotgun by his side. He was smoking a huge cigar; his face was pockmarked. The man was hugging a young girl wearing heavy make-up making her look older than she really was. "Sky, Razzy back off; it's my future partner, ol' Charlie."

"Partner! Not hardly! Look, I want my equipment back. I know you took it, and you leave my people alone or I will call the Feds down on you so fast you won't even be able to finish your cheap cigar," Charleton said angrily and meaning every word.

"C'mon Partner, what reason would I have to steal from you? I mean, we're gonna split everything fifty-fifty, right?" Jonesy mocked taking a puff off his cigar and blew it in Charleton's face; the girl laughed as only a lady can who is there just for the money.

"Look, you keep away from my people. I called the police and they're already looking for you, and I ain't joking about the Feds, back off or else."

Without warning the old man reached out the window and grabbed Charleton by the throat, causing his cigar to drop to the floor of the limo. The girl picked it up and started smoking it. "Nobody threatens Jonesy! Nobody! You call the Feds, the DA; you'll start picking up your employees in pieces. I didn't take your stupid equipment. Now get lost! You've got forty-eight hours to accept my offer, or you'll wish you never knew me," Jonesy said, pushing Charleton out of the window then yelling for Sky and Razzy as another young lady, dressed immodestly, came out of the pawn shop carrying a leather bag. She got in the car smiling briefly at Charleton, who was straightening his tie.

Charleton just stood in the street watching Jonesy's limo speed away. He finished adjusting his tie and coat, realizing the old man had quite a grip. As he walked over to his limo, he sighed as he remembered something his older brother told him, "a scared man can't gamble, and a running man can't fight." He knew they would meet again.

He got into the car trying to regain his composure after reassuring Joe he was alright. He told Joe to head to the office; Charlton arrived a little anxious, not afraid of Jonesy's threat, but knowing he was capable of carrying them out, especially those who were defenseless, so he debated about adding more security around his job sites and maybe his home.

It was 9:00 am when he arrived at his office. Elle greeted him warmly dressed in a brightly colored dress. She liked bright colors. "You've got a visitor; I sent her in."

"Who is it?" Charleton asked, reaching down to Elle's desk at a plastic box full of notes for him to respond to. He grabbed them as he walked toward his office door.

"You'll know, she's been here since I got here at 8:00."

"Fine," Charleton said as he opened his office door to find Rose staring out his office window as if she was thinking of something that would aggravate the person she came to see.

"Nice view, huh Rose?"

"Sorry Charleton, yes, it's a nice view. Your secretary said I could wait in here," Rose said, turning quickly toward him as she heard the door open.

"What do you need this morning? I'm rather busy. As angry as you were the other day when you rode to Sedalia with me, I thought you'd never come back." Charleton said sitting in his chair, he motioned for her to sit in front of him. As she did, he noticed she had a print-out of something next to her digital recorder that she had set on his desk while waiting for him to arrive.

"I guess I had a few more questions to ask you then I'll be out of your hair for good," Rose said calmly, feeling that Charleton felt nothing for her now; at least if he did, he wasn't saying anything. She turned the recorder on.

"Yes, go ahead, let's get this over with," Charleton said, leafing through notes on his desk, deciding who to call first, "How do you feel about women?" Rose asked directly, trying to look Charleton in the face. He didn't look up, except glancing at her adjusting the volume on the recorder; he looked back at his notes.

"What kind of question is that? I thought this article was about me?" Charleton said growing a little angry, finally looking up again.

"It is. I talked to some of your staff about you, women in particular. They say you're kind, considerate, and thoughtful. They said when they came to you about adding an on-site daycare, you said yes, and you had it up and running in just a few months. You added job sharing which they really like so they are able to spend more time with their families. That's commendable. However, when I talked to you the other day, you acted as if women were second-class citizens. I just want to know how you really feel, that's all."

"What? Now you think I'm an enigma? Look in the workplace — I feel perks make a person loyal, that's all. Daycare made sense, job sharing made sense, and it keeps the morale up and gets the work done. That's all, nothing more — nothing less. You know purple looks good on you," Charleton said, trying hard not to look at her long shapely legs and the rose embroidered on her blouse of lavender.

"You've talked a lot about my looks ever since I met you. It's as if you want more than just an interview," Rose said, seeing his eyes scan her body.

"I didn't say that at all. Oh, just forget it. I like women, okay? That's not a crime, is it?"

"No, but do you like your wife?"

"What's that supposed to mean?" Charleton asked, standing up. His eyes flashing, "I'm not going to discuss her, keep asking questions about her and I'll make you stop recording and call security to remove you from the premises."

"Let me read something, since you agreed to this article. I did a little research. I want you to listen for just a moment. I went over to see your family doctor, Doc Ellis. Boy, he sure says 'don't' cha know' a lot. It took a while, but the Doc did talk to me about visits to his office by your wife. I also went to the ER at the Med Center, the closest hospital to your house; because Doctor Ellis said some injuries he treated after someone else had worked on them. I did go to the DA, and they subpoenaed your hospital records. I have a copy here. Explain if you would, in 1981 there was an emergency room visit for a fractured jaw, Mrs. Magenta. In 1985 an ER visit to set a broken arm, Mrs. Magenta. In 1990 at Dr. Ellis' office broken bones in Mrs. Magenta's left hand. In 1993, Mrs. Magenta was treated for bruises around her right eye and most recently two broken ribs. I could go on for a long time, Charleton. Should I go on?" Rose asked, growing angry at the pattern of abuse.

Charleton sat back down, shocked to hear all this. He did not respond right away.

"Charleton, please don't tell me these injuries are all accidents by one clumsy woman. Maybe I should go on — you're speechless: a bruised thigh and a swollen left eye. You have a big problem sir, and if the rest of the press gets a hold of this, you can forget running for office. But the bigger issue here is the way you treated your wife. You really should be locked away in Sing Sing and have the keys thrown away," Rose said standing up as she watched him break down a little.

"Enough, enough! It seems like everyone is on my case about all this. They make me out to be a monster, the press and now you. I didn't hit her, I didn't. Turn off that tape! Turn it off now!" Charleton yelled, shaking his fist at her.

"Right now, you are a monster. You need help, Charleton. You really need to get counseling. Your wife really needs to get away from you. No woman deserves to be beaten, ever, for any reason. I…" before Rose could finish there were screams out in the hall that were loud and chilling.

"What in the world is going on?" Charleton asked running toward the door with Rose following, he opened it only to see Carl stumbling down the hallway with his face all bloody and his clothes soaked in blood. He collapsed on the white marble floor.

"Oh my! Carl! Somebody call 911!" Charleton yelled while running over to him. He fell on the floor trying to comfort him, getting bloody also. "Carl! Hang on buddy! Who did this? Who?"

Carl was barely able to open his eyes which were bleeding, along with his nose and mouth. "Sorry, sir. I let you down. I went to see Jonesy to give him his money back, what I had left, to try to make things right. He- he went berserk. He said to get a message to you, and I, I, I, am that message!... I'm sorry — so sorry."

"Hang on buddy, hang on," Charleton said as he and everybody on that floor just watched and prayed.

Part III
Chapter 20

Constance woke up Friday morning not feeling refreshed at all, because she had wrestled with whether to leave or stay, something she had done so many times before being abused.

As she had done so often when she was tossed between difficult decisions, she would decide to work in her flower gardens around the estate. They provided solace on occasion and helped her make better decisions. Her favorite flower garden was beside her swimming pool, with a sidewalk that branched off to a picnic area with marble tables and benches. Behind it was a large horseshoe shaped garden made of geodes. This was her favorite spot of all. The flowers were bright and pleasing peonies, violets and magnolias. Her favorite was Rosa Baron Girod de l'Ain, a Hybrid Perpetual rose which butterflies seemed to always flutter around.

She was on her knees digging in the soft soil when her son unexpectedly dropped by dressed for work. When she saw him, she got up to greet him, the knees of her pink stretch pants were dirty as well as the pink smock and her big pink sun hat tied under her chin was smeared with dirt also.

"Hello son. What a pleasant surprise. If I had known you were coming, I wouldn't haven't gotten so dirty. I do hate to be dirty except when it comes to my garden. The soil makes me feel a part of it!" Constance said standing up trying to hug and kiss her son without getting his brown French-cut designer suit dirty.

"Mom, I was thinking about you and was on this side of town checking on some land Dad wants to buy, and I thought I'd stop by." Ted said, being motioned by his mother to sit on the marble bench. The yellow canopy was fully out — keeping the sun off both of them.

Constance took her gloves off after putting her small spade down in the dirt. "Iced tea? It's fresh, Frances just brought it out." Constance said watching her son sit down with a reflection on his face like his mind was a world away. "Son, is something bothering you?"

"Yeah, sort of. You might not know this but before Teresa and I left we had a heart to heart about you and dad. We both agree he treated you pretty rotten through the years and …"

"But…" Constance motioned with her hands and dropped her head not wanting to discuss her husband at all.

"Mom, please let me finish. That night I went home, and I began to think, am I guilty of not treating women the way I should? All the talk shows and the tabloids really vilify any man who even talks to a woman wrong. I can't help but reflect on my own life."

"I know I should have told you earlier but, do you remember Tonya, the girl I dated a few years back? Well, everything was fine until she got pregnant. I don't know …" Ted said getting up and slowly walking around, "I don't know why — I guess I just wasn't ready for a kid at that moment. My plans were all set, and a kid right then would wreck everything. Mom, I blew up at her and kicked her out of the car — it was a horrible night, cold and rainy and I told her to abort the child. Ever since all this stuff with you and dad — I feel now I was so wrong. Her face was so bright and cheerful when she told me she was pregnant. She was so happy."

"Son, it's all right." His mother, Constance, hesitated then she stood up and hugged her son. Not concerned about the dirt now, she continued, "I know all about it."

"You do!? How? I hadn't spoken to her in about three years." Ted said pulling away from his mother but not looking at her in the face.

"She wrote me a letter recently, asking to be forgiven. Son, she never aborted the child."

"You mean?" Ted asked with a look of shock and disbelief like 'how could she have totally ignored his demands?'

"Yes, you have a son, a beautiful son a little over two years old. His given name is Theodore Lee Magenta, Jr., but Tonya calls him Pookie. He is the spitting image of you."

Ted sat down as if he'd just been hit over the head with a sledgehammer. He said, "Dang girl never listened to me anyway. A son, does dad know yet?"

"No — perhaps it might be best if you tell him. We're not on the best of terms right now," Constance said standing behind her son. She hugged his neck.

"Fine, a son — I have a son," Ted said suddenly growing reflective about how his life was starting to change.

"Yes, he's a fine boy. I think he's a little big for his age. He has black hair, brown eyes and your thick eyebrows, but his mother's nose and mouth. I met Tonya a few days ago. She wants our family to have a relationship with Pookie; like I said earlier that's what Tonya calls him."

"I guess I need to go talk with her and go see my son. Does she still live with her father?" Ted said standing and starting to leave.

"Yes, but maybe, my son, you need to write her a letter first. I have her address. I'm not sure how she feels about you. I watched her when she mentioned your name, there's still some hurt there." Constance said watching her son sigh, realizing he had indeed caused the hurt.

"Sure, I'll do that, mom, sure."

Chapter 21

Tonya had really enjoyed her visit with Constance to the point she was looking forward to the next one. Constance had told her when she left that she would make all of the arrangements for future visits.

It was mid-morning when her dad asked her to take a walk with him to their five-acre pond at the back of the estate. Her father, short and a little heavy, with lots of dark wavy hair, and the kindest dark eyes anyone had ever seen — had asked her to go with him so she did after pawning Pookie off on her younger sister Amber, who agreed with some protest.

The path to the pond led through some large oak trees and through some waist-high brush to a wide-open area. Around it was a rock-bottom pond, wooden deck, picnic table and a sandy beach with rocks scattered around — all man made. A flat bottom boat was flipped over on the bank. A gentle breeze rippled over the water.

"What a nice day, huh Dad?"

"Yes, it is, it's gorgeous. This is the day the Lord has made." Her father said, reaching down around his feet looking for a flat rock, "Hey, I bet I can skip a rock farther than you can."

"No way," Tonya said, looking for a flat rock of her own.

Tonya's father leaned over at an angle. He stretched his arm back and threw the rock at the surface of the water. "There, five — six — seven skips, beat that." He chuckled.

"Good, but not good enough, Pop." Tonya said bending over at her favorite angle. She stretched her arm and threw the rock as hard as she could — five, six, seven come on, one more, eight, eight! I beat you!" Tonya said, jumping in the air. "Finally! I beat you!"

"Yes, my rock throwing crown goes to you." Her father said, smiling. "Let's go sit down for a while. I want to talk to you about something. Let's sit here on the edge of the dock." They both moved there together, letting their feet dangle just above the water, hearing an occasional fish splash.

"I figured we didn't come here to skip rocks."

"No, Tonya you see, I've been praying a lot for you lately. At dinner last night you just seemed to have something on your mind. I was so glad to hear you met Mrs. Magenta. Boy, they're in all the newspapers, practically every magazine and on TV every day. My concern is — and I know in your heart you forgave Pookie's Dad, but I feel you still have some resentment toward him. You know that has to be dealt with, don't you?"

"I never could fool you, Dad. I tried not to be resentful, but sometimes, especially when I'm moody, I do feel resentful. I mean it was me who got up at 3:00 o'clock in the morning with Pookie. It was me who listened to him whimpering all night when his teeth were coming in and it was me who rocked him all night when he just wouldn't go to sleep. Sure you, Amber and even Zelda our maid helped me some. But I still felt so all alone," Tonya said gazing over the water watching the ripples move farther away from them.

"Yes, I know, and Pookie had colic for the first six months. No, you don't have it easy, and I praise you for being strong enough to be a single mom. My concern is that you shouldn't fill your heart with resentment and anger. You know God doesn't hold us accountable on how others react to us, but He does hold us accountable to how we react to others."

"What Teddy did was wrong, no doubt, but don't let the horrors of the past rob you of the wonders of the future. Pookie is your chief concern now," Tonya's father said, putting his arm around his daughter.

"Yes, you're right. If I wouldn't have slept with him, things would have been different. Yes, I must remember as Paul says in Philippians 3 in the middle of verse 14… 'but this one thing I do, forgetting those things which are behind, and reaching forth unto those things which are before…' How come, with all your help and the counselors, some days I feel I'm over Ted and the hurt — the next day it's an open wound?"

"It's not easy. Pray and let God know how you feel. Be honest with me now, do you still have feelings for Teddy? I thought he was a decent enough young man until he treated you so awful that night. But really, you shouldn't have been dating a non-Christian anyway. They just don't fit in with our belief system."

"Yeah, I learned my lesson the hard way. But, Dad, to be honest with you, with God and myself right now, I really don't know! I mean you're right up until then we got along well. We had our tiffs like any couple, but that was such a big nightmare that night. I just couldn't get over it that easily. At times I feel like moving on — other times I wish I was still with him despite what he did to me. 'Do I still love him?' To be honest, I'm not sure. Do I still want him in my life? Yeah, I probably do. Will he treat me like that again? Who knows? Dad, I really want to do the right thing. I want to move forward with my life. For Pookie's sake, I must. If the best thing is to leave Ted behind, then I must do that. You're right, as you often say: life isn't easy, is it? Choices — choices." Tonya said, standing up and stretching. Her Father did the same.

"You're a woman now, a lovely woman, but then again, as your father I'm prejudiced. You do need to decide how you feel about Ted. Do not let your heart get full of resentment and anger. When that happens you only destroy yourself. You know when I was taking counselor training, our teacher Ken Harlett, who we nicknamed Colonel Sanders because he looked just like him — only thinner — said anger is like a man who if he had welders gloves on and could pick up a handful of molten metal and sling it around in a crowd full of people it would scar a lot of them, some for life. Teddy scarred you and I'm not at all happy about that, but you, as a Christian, need to be better than the one that hurt you. Christ was. He didn't hurt the ones that hurt him, He forgave."

Tonya realizing her dad was right she hugged him and said "Thanks. Whenever I needed a true friend, you were always there. Promise me, Dad, you'll always be there for me, no matter what. Promise me."

With a big smile, Tonya's Father said, "I promise, of course, I promise."

CHAPTER 22

Carl was dead, and Charleton knew it as soon as the paramedics used a defibrillator on him with no response. Charleton watched them work on Carl, even as they hauled him off toward the Boone County Hospital. He followed in his limo in tears, anxious, hoping for a miracle. Less than 30 minutes after he arrived at the hospital, the doctor said it was just too late, the blood loss had been too severe.

He called back to the office and said anyone who needed the rest of the day off could do so without any repercussions. He stopped by home to clean up then headed back to work. He wanted to tell Constance, but she had gone out for another ride and her cell phone was not on.

As Charleton sat at his desk reflecting on his friendship with Carl, all the years they had together, now he was gone at only 64 years old. He had hinted at retirement to Charleton, but it was never taken seriously because Carl loved to work. He loved to build things just as Charleton did. Beyond Carl, he couldn't help but wonder what he was going to do about Jonesy. Immediately after arriving, as the police had rushed to the scene at his office, he had relayed Carl's last statement saying it was definitely Jonesy who had hurt him so horribly, and now he had caused his death, and because of that he had requested more security for his employees and worksites and also more regular patrols checking his home.

As he sat at his desk, he couldn't help thinking about how in less than 24 hours Carl went from life to death, from breathing to not breathing. For some reason he began to think about his own mortality. He saw the pain Carl was in and thought, "I sure wouldn't want to die that way — in agony."

"Die" Charleton thought, "I'm too young to die. I've got too much going for me." He leaned back and realized he probably should quit thinking about such morbid thoughts. Rose had not waited for his return, for which he was grateful. Though she was a "looker" she seemed to be stepping on his toes too.

"A monster — I'm a monster — Jonesy is the monster here. Sure, I've got problems, doesn't everybody?" Charleton's ramblings were interrupted by Elle as she buzzed in. "Sorry, Sir. Danner, Danner Coulter wants to see you."

"Send him in." Charleton said, really liking Danner, who was very straight forward and who seemed like a younger version of Carl.

"Sorry to bother you, Sir," Danner said with his head bowed — lost in sorrow.

"No problem, come in and have a seat," Charleton said motioning for Danner to sit down. He did and Charleton saw the redness in his eyes.

"Carl was a good man, wasn't he, Sir?"

"Yes, the best."

"I came here — I'm sorry to bother you, I just needed someone to talk to. The word came down that we could have the rest of the day off if we wanted to. I really didn't want to go home and be by myself — and well, I know you were really close to him." Danner said noticing Charleton's swollen face and eyes too.

"Yes, a tough loss. I knew him and Kate for years. Kate always seemed so gentle, a regular farm wife. I just couldn't believe she ran off with a knife salesman whom she met at a supermarket. I guess it takes all kinds. Carl didn't deserve the hand he was dealt."

"No, perhaps not, but life is what you make it." Danner returned softly.

"What do you mean, son?" Charleton said — leaning forward in his chair to listen.

"Well, Jesus didn't hurt anybody, but He was whipped, scourged and beaten — poked with a spear, yet He didn't curse back. He loved instead. Carl called me early this morning. He told me he'd been up all night, and he was thinking about his life, especially how recently he'd made some awful decisions; one was getting involved with Jonesy. It really bugged him that he didn't come to you and that he had treated you so badly when you had been nothing but good to him. He finally got down on his knees and cried out to God as he told me — the God he knew as a young boy. He said he made peace with God, and he wanted to make things right with you and the only way to do that was to take the money back to Jonesy. I told him maybe that wasn't the best thing to do, but he insisted. Well, that was a big mistake going to Jonesy, but a good thing going to God." Danner said, still feeling deep sorrow, suddenly feeling spiritual.

"Huh, he wanted to make things right with God? He was a good man, but it cost him his life. Where do you suppose he'll end up, Heaven or Hell?" Charleton said, a little shocked he was asking that particular question. He never considered himself a spiritual man, though he attended church occasionally on Easter, Thanksgiving and Christmas or when the kids were small, and they participated in church plays and pageants.

"Well, I believe if he truly got his soul right with God by confessing his sins and asking Jesus Christ to come into his life — then the minute he died he went to be with the Lord Jesus Christ in heaven."

"That's it! Don't you have to do anything to get into heaven? I mean being good, being a good person doesn't that count for anything? I mean, I give millions to charities every year! We financially support local churches. Constance and I have served soup at local churches!" Charleton said growing a little animated by the simplicity of it all.

"No, all that stuff is good, and I'm sure appreciated, but in the Bible, Ephesians chapter 2 verses 8 and 9 it says, 'By Grace are you saved through faith, that not of yourselves, it is the gift of God. Not of works, lest any man should boast." And in Acts chapter 4 verse 12 it says, "Neither is there salvation in any other, for there is none other name among heaven given among men, whereby we must be saved.' You see, Sir, we're all sinners. It says in Romans 3:23, 'All have sinned and come short of the glory of God'. It doesn't matter what you've done, you just have to accept Jesus and what He did for you when He died on the cross. He took our place. We sinned, not Him. He died for us. I didn't come here to preach but somehow, I think I needed to tell you this. Carl — what he did on earth will be just a memory but what he did for God will last forever. He helped me get through a few rough spots when I first started working here. I lost my mother. It didn't take him long to befriend me and encourage me. Yes, I know his faith waned toward the end, but he did care about the people around him and in that aspect, he was a lot like Jesus. Carl didn't care about what color or whether you were rich or not, he cared about you. He'd laugh with you; he'd cry with you. No, maybe he wasn't one to quote the bible, but I believe he lived its principles out. He knew it didn't matter what a person did, whether that person was good or bad, there was always room in his heart for you, Sir, that's what life is all about." Danner said realizing he had in fact been preaching but not intentionally. He watched Charleton. He seemed to be soaking in every word.

"Yes son, you're right. Listen, sorry to break this off, but I think I need to take care of a few things today. Thanks for stopping by; you're welcome anytime."

Chapter 23

Ted arrived home at his townhouse around 6:30 pm to find Melissa Carter dressed in a plush black and blue velvet button front duster jacket, black pants and strapped shoes, which were not on her feet but sitting beside her light green leather couch, sitting against a stylishly decorated French wallpapered wall, colorfully depicting Captain Cook's voyages.

She was smiling, showing a perfect movie smile. She shook her long golden hair, a habit she had wherever she went.

"Hi Baby! Great news! I got back at about 3:00 today. I got the part in my first movie starring Val Kilmer!" Melissa said, reaching both arms out to hug her future husband.

"Great. I'm so happy for you," Ted said, sitting down mechanically beside her after hugging her and kissing her on the cheek, instead of on her lips; Melissa didn't like that.

"Happy? Your face sure doesn't show it. You look like you've seen a ghost."

Melissa said, pulling Ted close to her, "What's going on?"

Ted sighed and said, "I really need to have a serious talk with you. First though, is supper ready?"

"No, I thought we'd celebrate. I made reservations at Kelper's. It's seafood night."

"Great! I do like their food! What time is our reservation?" Ted asked glancing in the dining room, seeing only a table with candles, flowers, and placemats of red, still hoping for supper somehow.

"Reservations are for 8:00 pm, we've got plenty of time. Tell me what's going on. You know how I hate to wait," Melissa said, adjusting her body to get more comfortable.

"Well, I guess I should have told you earlier, I mean the whole story anyway. Do you remember Tonya Green? The girl I dated before you?" Ted asked, hoping she'd remember and forget at the same time. Remember that she was his first love and forget that he ever told her anything in the first place.

"Yes, I remember her vaguely. You told me you broke up because of irreconcilable differences." Melissa said anxiously wondering where this conversation was leading.

"That's the one. I should have elaborated some, I mean, a lot." Ted said, slowing his speech down, as if he wanted to make sure he said the right thing. This delay bothered Melissa.

"C'mon, spit it out. What do you need to elaborate on?"

Ted got up from the couch and walked over to a set of mahogany lolling chairs, underneath an English George the Third Pier mirror, he breathed deeply, then said, "Today I visited my mother, she's been going through a lot, she was just on my mind. Anyway, I went over, and she told me Tonya had written a letter wanting to get involved with the family and believe me Melissa, I did not know this until that very moment, Tonya has a son, a two-year-old boy."

"What's that got to do with you? You told me you were never intimate." Melissa rather calmly believed Ted had always told her the truth.

"Well, he is my son. Mother met the boy, and he looks just like me. And yes, I really did sleep with her. I'm sorry I didn't tell you the whole story. I guess to me intimacy and having sex were not the same thing." Ted said, hanging his head down as he watched Melissa grow more animated from the shock of this revelation.

"No, I guess not. You said you never slept with her. Why? Why did you lie to me?" Melissa asked, her eyes starting to tear.

"I never planned it that way. The guys at Delta house got a little soused the night we met, we all decided to go to the movies. We saw these girls standing around. We figured they were in high school. Well, the guys dared me to see if I could score with the homeliest girl of the bunch and that was Tonya. I had thirty days. I was drunk and I took the dare. I know it was stupid."

"Stupid, you're right! A dare! What were you thinking? Women nowadays don't like stupid head games. Scoring like you're playing football! Obviously, you weren't thinking straight!" Melissa blurted back, hurt by this revelation.

"I'm sorry. Yes, I lied to you. I'm sorry, so sorry. I just don't like to talk about old girlfriends."

"You're sorry? Very sorry! To think I trusted you! How do I know I'm not one of your dares? How do you even know the child is yours? Couldn't she have been messing around with someone else?" Melissa asked, growing angry by the entire situation.

"No, I'm sure he is mine. She said I was her first. You see, we dated for about six months when she told me. I just wasn't ready for a kid. I was about to take the State Bar Exam — my life was going places — a kid was all wrong, the timing was bad. I told her to get rid of the child — I said I'd even pay for it, but…" Ted said, being interrupted by Melissa who got off the couch and walked over to Ted getting right in his face.

"You didn't bother to follow up to see if she went through with the abortion!? You didn't bother talking to her yourself?"

"No! I was angry! I didn't want anything to do with her! When I think back, she wrote me a lot, she called me. She even came over. I just wanted that part of my life to be over." Ted said, sighing regretfully at this episode.

"I just can't believe it. I can't believe you lied to me. I thought we had something real. I thought we could really get down to a heart — to — heart level and now this, a son! Right now! What an awful time for this to happen, I finally got the big break I've always wanted, and I guess now I'll be wiping noses. You ask me just to believe that you just found out today? What other secrets are you keeping from me Ted? Am I a dare too? Do you want me around just to score with? Do you still have feelings for Tonya? I mean you obviously slept with her. Do you have any other children I should know about?" Melissa said hotly, her face a bright red. Looking like an overfilled bicycle tire.

"Baby, it's not like that. You're the only woman for me, besides, that was over three years ago. If I had known I would have told you. I just didn't know. Believe me. And no, you are not a dare or just another score. You're the woman I want to spend the rest of my life with. Tonya, yes it started off as a big joke, but somewhere along the line I fell in love with her but that was a long time ago. She is nothing like you. It's the difference between a diamond and a cubic zirconium. She couldn't even tell the difference between Aram Khachaturian and Ruggew Leon Cavalio."

"What in the world does that have to do with sleeping with Tonya? Do *you* even know who those composers are?" Melissa asked, growing more irritated.

"Yes, Khachaturian did The Sabre Dance and Pagliacci was done by Leon Cavalio. There! The issue is I don't love Tonya anymore. I don't have feelings for her at all. I only want you. I messed up, okay? I did a stupid thing. How many times do you want me to say that? I know you and I talked about having kids when our careers were established, but I have a son — that's the issue now. What do we do about him? I'm sorry you're so upset."

"Don't you think I have a right to be!? Oh-oh, I trusted you. What do *we* do about him!? Not *we* — YOU! It's your mess! Boy, I think I really need to take a good look at my life."

"My mother went to see Pookie — that's what Tonya calls him. His real name is Theodore Lee Magenta, Jr. My mother suggested I write a letter to her first rather than visit. I guess she thinks Tonya is still a little sensitive about how I treated her. I do need to get the letter written soon. Mom gave me her address." Ted said, standing up and stretching seemingly exhausted by this entire conversation.

"A *little* sensitive!? That is the understatement of the year! I'd be a little sensitive too! Can I ask if you were going to visit or write your ex-girlfriend, your ex-lover without talking to me first? I suppose that's another little secret you were going to keep from me."

"Look, Baby," Ted said trying to calm her down by putting his arms around her — as he faced her, she backed away.

"Don't touch me! I don't know you anymore! You hide things from me and that stinks! That really stinks! Just put your jacket on and let's go eat. Boy, what a celebration this is going to be!"

Chapter 24

Dinner had not been good between Ted and Melissa because of her sudden lack of trust. Nothing tasted good. The calamari, crab legs, stuffed mushrooms a la carte all seemed to taste like they came out of an EASY-BAKE Oven.

Before the evening was over, they started to argue, much to the dismay of the other patrons who, by their faces, were glad to see them leave.

The drive home was silent. Neither one wanted to say anything for fear that another argument would ensue.

Arriving home, Melissa went upstairs to the bedroom. She made it plain that Ted should sleep downstairs on the couch. She tossed him a blanket and a pillow and then slammed the bedroom door.

Melissa had gotten dressed in her nightgown after taking an unusually long shower — for some reason the revelation of possibly being a stepmother, though she didn't understand everything, she felt unclean. She also felt betrayed for a lot of reasons. One, being according to Ted, she had been told that she was the first woman he had ever made love to, which now was a lie, though she never did reveal to him whether she was pure or not because she felt it was just part of her feminine mystique. She felt that the trust that was broken was so severe that she wondered if she could ever feel the same toward him again.

Melissa finally relaxed in her large adjustable air bed which she liked her side semi-soft. She always slept on the side of the bed away from the wall because she didn't like to be pinned in. for whatever reason; she began to think of her family.

She had known early that she was a direct descendent of French explorer Jacque Cartier who reached the Gulf of St Lawrence in 1534— many say he was the founder of Canada.

This exploring nature seemed to have worked its way through the centuries down to her because she loved traveling. She loved experiencing new things with people. She loved her mother who she remembered as a round woman who loved to dance around the kitchen making candies and cakes. She was a devout Christian who enjoyed attending church and preparing meals for church functions. Her dad thought church was only there for weak folks — folks who needed a crutch. He went only occasionally.

Melissa knew, however, when her mother suddenly died of a brain tumor, her father took it hard, so hard he left Montreal for America and settled in Washington, DC where he eventually met his second wife. Melissa accepted her but she couldn't really love her because she only seemed to care about little girls looking like Ascot queens all the time and church was only to be seen at. She did feel her new mother and father really loved each other so she made the best of it.

She used to watch them talk for hours and this was a source of comfort to her. They laughed and sang songs at the piano. She found out much later that her stepmom had won the Charles Ives Scholarship in music from the American Academy of Arts and Letters, which she used at the Berkeley College of Music in Boston, Massachusetts where she got her degree and she performed for years with the Boston Symphony, so as her stepmom had put it, she liked to be "around wealth and culture."

So, she wasn't all bad Melissa thought, but at the same time she had come along her stepmother had quit the Symphony. She had no children of her own so Melissa became her perfect guinea pig to enter society.

Melissa didn't mind some of it but being made up to look eighteen when she was seven and going from town to town entering beauty pageants with hairdos bigger than the women of the 60s. She was wearing clothes much too tight and sexy for a child which made her feel a little strange sometimes. Most of the girls in the contests would have rather been home playing hopscotch or Twister.

It seemed her whole life was looking beautiful for some judge whom she never knew. Her father didn't particularly like it, but he just stayed out of it. Why, once they flew clear down to Texas just so she could learn how to talk, walk and have her make-up done by the leading producer of beauty pageant winners in the United States.

Yes, she had won her share of beauty pageants, county fairs and state fairs. In 1999 she was even the second runner up in the Miss America pageant. Now she felt all of this was great on some level but all she ever wanted to do was act.

Her favorite actresses were Sigourney Weaver for her strength and character and Nicole Kidman for her charm and beauty. She loved Nicole in "Moulin Rouge." She studied acting whenever she wasn't doing anything else. She loved being someone else, even if it was just for a little while.

She didn't have to look perfect like she did when modeling, but her family had other plans. They thought Hollywood was full of silicon injected ladies with no character or judgment. They went round and round until she turned 21, which she had two years ago, so now she was pursuing her dreams.

Her dreams seemed to consume her thoughts as she continued to lie quietly on the bed, smashing herself deeply into her white satin covered pillows. She couldn't help but think to herself, "My career is ruined! A stepmom? Am I ready for that? I mean — finally I get to do something I always wanted to and now I have to be a mother, but do I have to? Can I really trust Ted anymore? Do I want a relationship where I can't trust the man I'm with? What if two years down the line another kid pops up?"

"What about the mongrels in Hollywood who just feed on dirt? They find out about this I'm ruined before I get started!"

"Yes, I love Ted. He has shown a lot of love to me, but now it all seems to be changing for us, for me."

"Believe me, believe me, that's all he says but how can I? You don't forget that you slept with someone, especially your first time! Believe him? No way! Wait, I only have his side of the story. Maybe I need to pay Ms. Tonya Green a visit. No, I shouldn't; that really shows I don't trust him, then again, the trust is already broken. Maybe I can get a better understanding talking woman to woman."

"That's it. I'll have a talk with Ms. Tonya. He told me when we first started dating that her father was the Reverend Green on TV. Maybe I can find out where she lives by talking to the TV station or somebody, anyway, I'll find out where she lives and talk to her and find out the whole truth."

With these thoughts Melissa finally relaxed, realizing tomorrow she would find out what Tonya was really like, not just what Ted thought of her. "After all," Melissa said to herself, "she couldn't be all that bad if Ted once made love to her and once even thought about marrying her. We'll have a heart-to-heart talk, maybe that will help straighten things out."

She finally fell asleep.

Back downstairs, Ted tried to sleep on the couch and could not. He tossed and turned like he had an upset stomach that no Tums could cure. He knew he never liked Melissa being mad at him because it made him jumpy and irritable.

He felt he had done right by telling her the truth, but he knew he had done wrong by lying to her about the intimacy of his relationship with Tonya. He had never seen her so upset. He felt like she was ready to dump the whole plate of stuffed mushrooms at the restaurant on his head. It had been the worst dining out experience he had ever had. He regretted that the maître d' had seated them at a center table rather than off in some dark corner where their actions could be somewhat hidden.

Ted sat up on the couch thinking about the drive home which was horrible. The utter silence was driving him crazy. He knew whenever she rode in his Jaguar and turned toward her window, that she was highly perturbed. He knew he dearly loved Melissa. He often told her she was his dream girl, his belle femme because she was by far the most beautiful woman he had ever known. She was, quite simply, gorgeous. Whenever she stepped into a room every eye, men and women both, stopped to stare. She had the flawless beauty of Marilyn Monroe with all the charisma of a young Debbie Reynolds. Ted knew with all her breeding she had developed into the quintessential lady and even though some thought she was a high brow, she was never too busy to speak kindly to people who recognized her from runways, magazine covers and TV ads that she had done through the years.

As he sat up and fidgeted for a while, everything seemed to be changing in his life; the issues with his mom and dad and now having a son. He knew he dearly loved Melissa, but Tonya kept flashing in his mind like a yellow light in the center of a small town.

"A son," Ted said to himself. "I have a son. Someone, as mom says, looks just like me. Maybe he'll grow up to play basketball, baseball, or like me, play rugby. I have a son."

Ted swallowed hard as he realized the gravity of it all, the responsibility and wondering whether he had really gotten Tonya out of his system. He knew he didn't think about her very much but every once in a while, while channel surfing, he'd see her father, Reverend Green and then he would reflect on her. He knew he could never forget the tenderness of their first time being intimate. Being involved with Melissa was something lasting, not something fleeting.

Ted knew that Tonya could never touch Melissa's outer beauty, but her simple trusting nature appealed to him. Ted knew that Tonya was much more the country girl who liked county fairs, playing horseshoes, going fishing and skipping rocks. All of which his family rarely did, preferring to pursue activities that deemed to fit their social status. Ted knew that Tonya could be a bit clingy, but she never, ever got tired of telling him how much she truly loved him, which heard mostly only from his mother, who told him often how she felt, but his dad didn't believe that men should be mushy about love.

He knew he liked to hear Tonya saying it, though he had been the one that initiated the love making. She had wanted to wait but he seduced her, convincing her they both wanted each other, so she gave in.

"But where did all my love for her go the day she told me she was pregnant?" Ted muttered to himself. This thought had plagued him off and on since that night. But he thought after meeting Melissa all this had nearly faded from his memory; but now all that happened that night was coming back again.

As the hour got later, he laid back down and tossed and turned, adjusting the couch pillows for his head. No matter which way he turned the green tasseled pillows, he couldn't rest. He finally got up and walked around, went to the kitchen for a drink of soda and nibbled on a baby carrot. He sat down on a chair at the dining room table and noticed the large clock shaped like a sunburst showed it was 2:30 am.

He rested his head on the table in his arms hoping he could just go to sleep, but he couldn't. He mumbled to himself, "what am I going to do about Tonya and what am I gonna do about Melissa? One thing about it, Tonya never got mad at me — never, but Melissa! Wow, she can be a real wildcat sometimes."

Ted got up and walked to his home office area with its roll top desk beside a computer desk with a PC, computer books, CD-ROMs and DVDs all neatly stacked. He thought about tinkering around on the internet but decided not to.

As he sat down at his desk, he saw a pad and paper there where a few days ago he and Melissa had started on the preliminary ideas for their June wedding, even though it was over 10 months away. He never liked to wait until the last minute.

He sighed and noticed the desk clock with gold golf clubs on the side now registered 2:45 am. He felt groggy but couldn't relax. He removed a medium point, blue Bic pen and started doodling. For some reason he drew a church and a wedding cake. He scratched it out and said, "That's not even a certainty anymore."

He continued to think about both women, he knew exactly what Melissa thought about the whole situation, but it had been three years since he had seen or heard from Tonya.

"I must know how she feels. If she hates me, I'll know. If she loves me, I'll know. She probably can't possibly love me after the way I treated her the way I did. I wish there was a way I could tell her how I feel before we meet. How? How? Is there any way she could know that my behavior that night was just an aberration?"

"Maybe, wait; maybe that's it! Mother said I should write her first. Yes, that's it! Should I tell Melissa? If I do, she'll probably go ballistic on me. If I don't, she'll still go ballistic on me. She'll ask, why am I writing letters to my ex. Why?"

"Wait, though. Maybe Tonya will write me, or we can see each other face to face and we can express our feelings, then I can tell Melissa. Boy, whichever way I go someone's not going to be happy. What do I have to lose? Only the most beautiful girl in the world. What is it they say? 'If true love was meant to be, set it free; if it comes back, it was meant for thee.'" Ted said, smiling to himself. He finally got the letter written after three starts. He didn't proofread it the last time. He put it in an envelope and put it in the inside of his work briefcase. Then he laid down on the couch and fell asleep, seemingly at peace with himself.

Chapter 25

Jonesy had always tried to be a fair businessman as long as he set the rules according to himself. However, he was so offended at Charleston's rebuff that he was going to ruin him, no matter what it took, even if he didn't bow to his wishes.

He felt his huge estate in a remote area Northwest of Columbia was impregnable with its red brick front and circle driveway, all surrounded by a tall electric fence and guards. The police had paid him a visit but found no stolen items nor any proof that he killed Carl, but the harassment alone got Jonesy ticked off more than he had been in a long time.

Sitting at his round maple breakfast table, set with fine silver and china all resting on a red tablecloth, he was eating alone, drinking most of his breakfast.

Sky and Razzy were in the room sitting on the windowsill chest-seats, painted to match the beige criss-cross patterned wallpaper.

Jonesy was prone to doing things that never made sense. He had been a criminal ever since he could remember. He was now 75 years old and wanting more of everything. Nothing could really satisfy him. Without warning he jumped up and threw his whiskey glass at a painting on the wall of dogs playing poker.

"The cops, I'm sick of them snooping around here. I want Magenta's fortune. We get that and we can all be outta here, we can all retire! Right fellas?"

Sky and Razzy chimed in, "Right boss."

"Am I not a reasonable man, fat boy?" pointing at Razzy.

"Sure boss, you're reasonable." Razzy said, smiling sheepishly.

"Then what's the problem? Doesn't Charlie get it? His company is worth ten billion dollars! I only want half, isn't that reasonable?"

"Yes," Sky and Razzy chimed in again.

"Then why ain't I got it? I'm tired of playing games. I hope they get the message I sent them. Next time it's gonna be worse."

"Come here, you," Jonesy said pointing to Sky. Sky hesitated, not sure what his boss was about to do, but he came toward him anyway and Jonesy reached out and grabbed him by the throat with both hands.

"I had him in my grip the other day. I should have squeezed all the life out of him then. Squeeze and squeeze and squeeze." Jonesy said, squeezing Sky's throat so that his face was turning colors.

"Boss, let go, he's on our side!" Razzy said, running to his friends' aid, pulling at his boss's hands until he finally let go.

"Ahh, look, you go talk to ol' Charlie one more time. Tell him he'd better become my partner or else! This time I'll take care of the 'or else' myself. Got it, fellas? I want to leave this town. I want an answer by 12:00 noon Friday — now go!"

Sky rubbed his throat and looked at his boss with fear and then he quickly left the room with Razzy, who watched his boss in anger turn the whole table over, breaking dishes and glasses.

Jonesy yelled, "Charleton Magenta, your day has come! No one man should be that rich! No man!"

Chapter 26

Constance had decided to meet at Tonya's home where she resided at her father's estate. It was much smaller than hers but very well kept.

It was midafternoon on a Monday. When Constance arrived, she was greeted by an older lady with a slight hunchback, a small frame, white hair and the happiest face anyone had ever seen.

"Hi, I'm Zelda, the housekeeper. Tonya is expecting you. She is just down the hall in Pookie's toy room," Zelda said smiling, walking slowly leading the way.

"Thanks, I'm Constance Magenta."

"Yes, I know, Tonya's told me a lot about you. Just for the record, I don't believe all the garbage they're saying about you. I never judge people by the outside; it's the heart that matters. I've seen all the good you've done in the community. You must have a great heart to do all that. Here we are. Pookie, you have a visitor."

Pookie looked up to see his grandmother and ran toward her, stopping short of rolling a ball bigger than his head at her. Constance bent down rolling the ball back while setting her purse down on the hardwood floor.

"If you need anything, just yell for me." Zelda said as she left, then turned back and continued, "Mrs. Magenta, I'll keep you in my prayers."

Constance still bending down turned and mouthed "thank you" to Zelda and quickly turned her attention to Tonya, who was sitting at a child sized desk in front of a kid sized bookshelf, full of books.

"Hi Constance! Boy, Pookie sure keeps this room a mess. Cars, trucks, games, balls, watch your step. What a mess all over the floor," Tonya said, choosing a book and heading toward Pookie who was still playing ball with Constance, who rather ungraciously got down on her knees to play like a toddler.

"He's so much fun." Constance said, rolling the red and white speckled ball toward him after glancing at Tonya, noticing she had chosen the book "Cinderella" to read. She watched Pookie pick the ball up and start to roll it back when he tripped over a large hand driven motorcycle. He started to cry a little, but Constance swooped over and picked him up.

"There, there, you're all right. You're a big boy now." Constance said, getting up awkwardly with him in her arms. She walked over, trying not to trip, to a yellow and white painted toy chest with a padded top. Pookie seemed to like her holding him.

"How have you been Tonya? Oh, he's such a cutie. All the girls are going to be after him one day."

"Please don't make him grow up too soon." Tonya said, getting up from the blue Playskool desk and walking over toward them. Pookie saw this and scrambled off his grandmother's chest and ran to his mother.

"Mommy, Mommy." Pookie said, feeling even more secure in her arms. Tonya then went to a large wooden rocking chair next to a corner full of stuffed toys: giraffes, lions, bears and a purple dinosaur.

"He might be getting a little tired. He didn't have his morning nap. There on the shelf, behind, by all his Hot Wheel cars, can you hand me his sippy cup?" Tonya asked, pointing to the cup to the right of Constance. She tried to reach it sitting down, but she couldn't so she got up and retrieved it for Tonya, it was about half full of blue liquid which Constance figured was probably Kool-Aid. Pookie immediately reached for the cup and started to drink.

"This is his favorite." Tonya said smiling.

"Looks like it," Constance said, watching him drink. She then scanned the room. It had a small daybed along one wall and pictures of clowns and brightly colored balloons above it.

"So how are you today, Constance?" Tonya asked, rocking back and forth listening to Pookie singing as he tried to fight sleep after pushing the cup away.

"Fine, better, I guess. I really do enjoy these visits. I'm so glad you asked me." Constance said lowering her voice seeing that Pookie's eyelids were getting droopy.

"I do too. Excuse me; I'll put him on his bed, he might go to sleep, and we can talk. He does sleep soundly." Tonya said stopping the rocking chair and putting the cup on the floor, she slowly got up and put Pookie on his back in the daybed — he sleeps well that way. She patted his stomach and chest as he stirred some as she first laid him down, then she heard him breathe soundly, almost snoring.

"I believe he'll sleep for a while," Tonya said, going over to Constance who had walked over to the windows of the playroom to see the pool being cleaned by an elderly man in a short sleeve white shirt and white cap. He was removing a few early dry leaves that had floated into the pool.

"Leaves are falling early this year. Seasons are starting to change already." Constance said feeling a little sad, perhaps feeling that her life was changing too.

"Yes, nothing remains the same. You look better today. You don't seem so uptight." Tonya said standing beside her, watching the pool man.

"Yeah, it's still hard to be honest. I hate being in the media so much. Reporters are calling me all the time wanting me to tell my side of the story. It seems if they can't speak to me personally, they talk to my friends who sometimes embellish the truth. Oh, I wanted to tell you, I did talk to Ted; he does know about his own son."

"Oh, he does," Tonya said as if she had just swallowed something sour. She sat on the toy chest and continued, "I guess that's good."

"You don't sound very happy."

"Well, I guess, it's just that I don't know how I feel about him. I mean the other day dad and I talked about this very issue. Sometimes the hurt I feel is still so real. Have you ever been hurt that way before? A hurt that is so deep that it goes clear down to the very bottom of your heart, the very bottom?" Tonya asked, reaching over and pulling the rocking chair over for Constance to sit in.

Constance answered as she sat in the rocker, "Yes, I've been there. Funny I noticed the book you picked out, "Cinderella". In all these years I wondered if she really did live happily ever after. I mean, after all she had the gorgeous prince, the palace and all the money she could ever want. I wonder if she was ever really happy." She leaned back trying to imagine the scene in her head.

"Funny you should bring up happiness. Dad's been leading a Bible Study about joy and happiness on Wednesdays. You're always welcome to attend. It's at Victory Faith Church, our church, at 7:00 pm. It's great, but Dad was saying that happiness depends on outside circumstances, such as having everything you want, but joy is much deeper, it comes from within the soul. It doesn't care what's going on — on the outside, it's secure knowing that God will never leave you or forsake you. That no matter where you go or what you do, He will always love you."

"That would be nice. I guess, Tonya, to be honest I'm just not happy. I mean if anyone was Cinderella, I was. I didn't have the best start in life, but I did marry the prince. I do have the palace; I do have all the money I will ever need but there is still a hunger in me, and I don't know for what. Yes, I do, I want to be loved. I want to be held, I want to be called special, I want ...." Constance started to cry, "I'm so sorry; I didn't come over to babble like some child. If I'm not careful I'll wake Pookie."

"You're not babbling. Besides, it's good to get that stuff out. What you have is a hunger, restlessness. In school we studied St. Augustine, and he called it 'Corinquetum: a restlessness at the heart of our being that drives us in the search for what is true whether in life or love…' You've got that restlessness, that hunger for the truth, for love and the only solution is God, Constance. Nothing or no one can ever fill that void inside of you. Your husband can't, your kids can't, and your riches can't. Only God can satisfy," Tonya said watching Constance retrieve a white monogrammed kerchief from her purse. Before she closed it, she said, "Oh, I almost forgot this; Ted dropped this letter by the house for you when I told him I was coming to visit you today."

"Thanks," Tonya said looking at the letter quickly then setting it beside her on the bench.

"Do you know Jesus Christ? I mean, really know him?"

"Well, when I was fifteen, I went forward when they asked if anybody wanted to accept Jesus, so I did. I was baptized two weeks later. I guess that's what you mean."

"Yes, but did you ask Him to forgive you of your sins and come in and make a new creation in Him? Did you ask Jesus to totally take control of your life, so that He could become your Lord and Savior?" Tonya asked boldly, leaving the bench and kneeling beside the rocking chair.

"No, I don't believe that happened, but I do try to live a Christian life — I guess I just couldn't understand two things. One was how such a loving God would allow…" and as if she was frozen stiff by a shot of cold air, she burst into such heavy tears she couldn't finish her sentence.

"Allow what? Constance? What?"

"How could a loving God allow my Father to kill my mother and allow me to be beaten," Constance said crying horribly, barely able to be understood.

"Get beaten? What are you saying?" Tonya asked, reaching up and putting her arms around Constance.

"Beaten! My husband beats me! He beats me!" Constance said crying so loudly that Pookie started to awaken. As she noticed this, she said, "sorry to wake him up. I ruin everything."

"No, you don't. I had no clue that happened to you and that your husband beats you. You don't have to put up with that. Anybody who beats up on another, especially a spouse, that's not love. Oh, Constance, I never knew you were in this much pain. I'll help you. I'll be here for you, I really will." Tonya said as she embraced Constance while she cried and cried and cried.

Chapter 27

Tonya was horrified at Constance's confession concerning her childhood and her present life with her husband and his violent tendencies. She had given her the number to the local women's shelter and stressed to her that she should contact them immediately. Right now, the best thing she could do is to leave her husband and get her own life in order. She needed to work on healing herself from the inside out. Tonya had also said that prayer and reading the bible would help her immensely.

Tonya knew they had come together that day as friends, but they parted as sisters.

However, it wasn't even three hours later when she received another visitor, whom she had never seen in person, but she did realize she had seen her before. The lady standing in front of her now was tall and lean and wearing dark glasses on a face that was literally without a single blemish. She was dressed in an all-black rather tight outfit with open Xs down the leg that revealed her bronze skin. Her hair was long and gold, drifting down past her shoulders. She had large gold earrings that matched three bracelets on each wrist.

Tonya had been escorting Pookie to the kitchen when she heard the doorbell, she asked Zelda to watch her son, and she would answer the door.

"Yes, may I help you?"

"Yes, sorry to come unannounced. Are you Tonya Green?" the lady asked, shaking her hair as she always did.

"Yes."

"You're prettier than Ted said," the woman said, mumbling to herself.

"What was that you said? Something about Ted?" Tonya asked. "That's all I heard. Won't you please come inside?"

"Thank you. Yes, I did say Ted, Ted Magenta to be more specific. I'm his fiancé. We're planning on tying the knot next year. Sorry, I didn't introduce myself, I'm Melissa Cartier," she said, staring at Tonya's face, which had a baffled look of why she had come over to see her in the first place and also a look of regret that Ted had obviously moved on without her.

"Congratulations. Oh, wait, I didn't think I knew you when I first saw you but aren't you in those Guess Jeans and Victoria Secret ads? You must get chilled, no more clothes than you wear." Tonya said the last sentence under her breath as she shut the door behind Melissa.

Melissa just smiled thinking of saying a silly response as she read her lips, she moved on to the reason she had come.

"I'm glad you recognize me. I won't take too much of your time. I need to talk to you, let's say woman to woman, about Ted."

"Why? I mean I've been out of Ted's life for three years now and you have a relationship with him, not me. I guess I still don't understand why you're here?" Tonya asked honestly, seeing Melissa a little animated.

"Look, can we talk some place privately please? It's really important to me, okay?" Melissa asked, her face a little flushed by this mild resistance from Tonya.

"I guess so. Zelda, come here a minute please," Tonya said, turning her head and calling toward the kitchen.

Melissa looked in the same direction toward an elderly lady dressed in black, her favorite color, with a white shawl and a white "bun" cap on her silver hair. Her smile was radiant as she walked with Pookie, who let go and ran between his mother's knees as they all stood in the blue and white vestibule, trimmed in pastel blue.

"Yes Tonya," Zelda said softly, watching Pookie play hide and seek around his mother's legs with the stranger in front of her.

"Zelda, this is Melissa, or would you prefer Ms. Cartier?" Tonya asked, watching Melissa's jaw drop as if she couldn't believe this was Ted's son.

"Boy, he's got those Magenta eyes doesn't he and look at that dark curly hair. Oh, Melissa is fine," she said, wanting to bend down as most people do with kids playing hide and seek, but she didn't quite know what to do.

"Hey, Pookie say hi to the pretty lady," Tonya said, reaching down and pulling him up to her hip. He just smiled then smashed his face into his mother's chest, then flirted with Melissa, as little children often do.

"Zelda, oh Melissa, this is Zelda our housekeeper," Tonya said, pausing as Zelda nodded hello, then she continued, "Would you please watch Pookie for me? Melissa and I are going out by the pool for a while. Would you like something to drink?" she asked Melissa.

"No, I'm fine, thanks," Melissa said respectfully, watching Tonya give Pookie back to Zelda. He fussed a bit but with some coaxing from his mother, they both left.

"Ummies, do you want some ummies, Pookie?" Zelda asked, sounding like a toddler herself as she smiled at both women and went toward the kitchen.

"C'mon this way Melissa," Tonya said walking straight down the hallway where two white lattice framed doors opened to a huge kidney shaped pool trimmed in white and blue tile. At about the middle section of the pool off to the side sat a Jacuzzi made for six people.

There were also small flower gardens, some with small trees growing in them. Off to the left was an area with a few white wrought iron chairs, some loungers with bright flower cushions of yellow which matched the open canopies.

It wasn't particularly hot that day though there was a slight breeze, just enough to make the white tassels at the end of the canopies move.

The water in the pool was clear and looked blue against the blue tile.

"Here, if that's all right?"

"Fine, nice pool, the water looks so refreshing," Melissa said, staring at it as she walked by. She sat across from Tonya whose face was still showing a certain amount of discomfort. She was still asking herself why Melissa had come.

"How long have you been a model? Come to think of it, I've seen you on the covers of Vogue, Seventeen and Bride."

"Yes, you're right; also, I've been on the cover of Elle and Marie Claire. Oh, I've been at it ever since I could walk, but it seems like, but to tell you the truth all I wanted to do was act. As a matter of fact, I just got back from a screen test to star opposite of Val Kilmer in his next movie, and I got the part!" Melissa said, gloating a bit.

"That's great! I wish you all the best. He is so handsome. I loved him in 'Batman Forever' and 'The Saint'," Tonya seemed genuinely happy for her, but felt that Melissa hadn't come to discuss Hollywood. She paused, then continued, "What is it you wanted to discuss? Did Ted send you?"

"No, why would you think that? To be blunt Ted and I had a big fight a few nights ago because out of nowhere he says he has a two-year-old son. He said he didn't know until a few nights ago. Which is funny, when we first started dating, he told me that you and him never slept together, duh — how can he have a son if that were true? I know this might sound awful, but I came to get the truth right from 'the horse's mouth' so to speak. I'm really ticked off at him." Melissa said, putting her purse down on the table then jumping up as her anger swelled at the idea of rehashing the whole scene with Ted.

Before Tonya had a chance to respond she started talking again, but she noticed how calm and collected Tonya was and that bothered her some. Then she continued, "I got back from California Saturday, all ready to celebrate with Ted. I made reservations at Kepler's, I bought a new outfit, got an appointment at the hairdresser and Ted hits me with this bombshell. I just got the biggest break of my life and now this."

"Melissa, please sit down. You're working yourself up. Yes, I know you must feel hurt, relax." Tonya said, reaching across the glass table and trying to reach for Melissa's hand in an effort to help her settle down. Melissa pulled her hand away and her face was still flushed.

Tonya smiled kindly with reassurance that she understood the emotions that had been flowing through her.

"Relax, Ted did not know until Saturday. That's when his mother told him. She visited earlier today. He had stopped by her house to talk with her, and she told him then, but it's not that he didn't have the opportunity. To answer your other question, yes, I'm afraid he did lie to you. Unfortunately, we slept together more than once. I say unfortunately because we weren't married. You see three years ago I …" Tonya said, being interrupted by Melissa, who jumped up again.

"What's that have to do with anything? Marriage is nothing but a piece of paper — doesn't everybody live together first? Look, the fact is he says he never slept with you at all, you say more than once. What's going on?" Melissa asked, walking around again, growing angrier all the time.

"Why are you so angry? Did you come here expecting a scorned woman? When Ted found out I was pregnant I thought he would be happy, instead he blew up. He called me horrible names. It was not a good night for me. It was raining and he kicked me out of the car, knee deep in mud but through all this I felt God's comfort, giving me strength. I must have cried a million tears that night. But with God and my dad's help, I got things right with my Lord and Savior, Jesus Christ." Tonya paused and took a deep breath, as if she were blowing a toy sailboat across the water.

"I tried, God knows how many times, to contact Ted to tell him I was going to have the baby, he wanted no part of me or his son. I called him; I wrote him, and all of the letters came back unopened. I even stopped by his house, but I got nowhere with him, so I chose to go on with my life."

"I became a single mom. With my dad and my sister Amber's help, and most importantly God's, I knew Pookie, and I would make it."

"It wasn't until recently that I thought about trying to reach out to Ted and his family again, and I started with Constance."

"Melissa, I know it hurts to be lied to, but it's a greater hurt to carry anger around." Tonya said stoically as Melissa slowly came over and stood right in front of Tonya and stared into her soft, kind face.

"How can you sit there and be so calm? If he kicked me out in the mud and called me names, he'd have one heck of a fight on his hands. I'm not just a Barbie doll, you know! I can be a real ..." Melissa said, wanting to say something else, but she saw on Tonya's face such love and peace seemingly about everything, that she went over and sat down calming some.

"How can I be so calm? In Matthew 5:44 Jesus said, 'But I say unto you, love your enemies, bless them that curse you, do good to them that hate you, and pray for them which despitefully use and persecute you'."

"I won't say that I don't struggle with that issue, because Ted hurt me bad, but I pray for him and wish him all the best. He has found you and I wish you both all the best. I don't hate Ted either. I just want him to have a relationship with his son and a relationship with the Lord Jesus Christ."

"I'm not the same naïve girl I was three years ago. I'm a 'New Creation' in Christ — old things have passed away."

"Yes, I still say it was unfortunate that I disobeyed God. Marriage is His only plan for intimacy between a man and a woman, but I was blessed with a little boy," said Tonya.

"Funny you mentioned marriage, on TV the other night they had a special about the wedding vows and commitment." Melissa said.

"You're right, like you said earlier, a lot of people do live together, but that still doesn't make it right," Tonya responded softly.

"On one of the services on TV they said, 'Heavenly Father, we have these people who have accepted these vows of marriage, grant them grace, courage, love and loyalty and the consistency and faith to maintain these vows to the end'. Now, I'm not sure every word is exact, but love, loyalty and faith are so important, and I believe they are the essence of being with someone. I'm sure you're hurt because all of these have been broken with Ted. I'm sure I've probably said more than I should, having just met you and all but, Melissa, God loves you so much he died so that you could live. One person said, 'He hung up for all your hang ups'."

"This is just a suggestion that worked for me three years ago. The Bible says, 'Cast all your care upon Him, Upon Jesus, for He cares for you'."

"I believe Ted is not really the issue here, but rather how you feel about yourself," Tonya said, reaching her hand out to Melissa again — who met Tonya's hand halfway this time, grasping it firmly.

Melissa looked at Tonya seeing her soft smile, she smiled back briefly, then her anger seemed to lessen and slowly she started to cry. She spoke with brokenness in her voice, "Yes, it's about me, and no, you haven't said too much. You see I spent my whole life parading in front of judges whether it was a beauty pageant, a talent show, a county fair, state fair, or the Miss America pageant, it was all the same. I felt it was all about the way I looked, not how I felt, not what I thought as I got older and did runway. Whether it was Fendi or Ralph Lauren, it didn't matter; all the flash bulbs didn't care about how I felt. You don't know how many nights I cried myself to sleep just wanting someone to hold my hand, tell me they cared. Sure, I dated but I felt the guys just wanted to brag that they've been out with a Super Model."

"Ted was the first man that I thought really wanted to know me for me, for who I really was inside. I felt he fell in love with the real me. I thought I found my soulmate. He always encouraged my acting. He was in the audience when I auditioned with the Lincoln Center Theater in New York and the Mark Taper Forum in LA, I got accepted with Mark Taper and as they say, the rest is history. I was finally doing what I always wanted to do."

"I could be anybody from St Joan to Grandma Moses. I didn't have to always be this "Ascot Queen" parading around in satin and lace. I finally felt free."

"Ted made me feel so special — then I get my big break — and this happens. You know it's like when your car has been sitting for a while and you come out to see a spider web on it — one of those big ones that stretch the length of the antennae and the way the light hits it you can see all the lines and designs — see all the work the spider put in — but you know you can't have a spider living in your car, so then with one swipe of your hand all the spiders hard work is gone in an instant. That's what I feel like. I feel like that spider, my whole life seemed to be wiped out when he lied to me about you and him. The kid issue I probably could have dealt with if I'd have known earlier, some women can love another woman's child and some can't."

"Oh Tonya, sometimes I feel like I have everything, yet like I have nothing. I see you and you're so calm, your face is glowing like a candle on a dark night. You're nothing like Ted said you were. You're a woman of character. I'm not sure about this Jesus, but I want to find out more about him. Please." Melissa said, now very reserved. She started to cry not even realizing that Tonya had already gotten up and walked over to her, to embrace her and begin to silently pray for her. Then speaking softly, "Melissa,

Jesus can really help your life. All you have to do is ask Him to forgive you for all your sins and to come into your heart. All you have to do is call out to Him. He will change your life and wash you whiter than snow. He died so you could live. He is our sacrifice for sin. He loved you, me, and everyone while we were yet sinners. Would you like me to pray with you, to ask Jesus into your heart?"

Melissa said 'yes' softly, her eyes blurred from crying, she continued, "yes, I want what you have. I want peace and joy. I want Jesus to come live in my heart. I know I haven't lived right. I have been a sinner. I am so sorry. I want to change my life. I need a change in my life. I want to feel like I am loved from the inside out, if Jesus can do that — that's what I want! I'm not much on the prayer thing, so can you pray for me?"

"Gladly. Lord Jesus, Melissa is crying out to you today. She wants you to come live in her heart. She wants to be a New Creature in Christ. You say in John 5:13, 'These things I have written unto you that you believe in the name of the Son of God, that ye may know that ye have eternal life,' Melissa wants eternal life, she wants to be forgiven. She is sorry for her sins and wants to feel what Peter declares in Acts 3:19, 'Repent ye therefore, and be converted, that your sins may be blotted out, when times of refreshing shall come from the presence of the Lord' ... Refresh her right now, Lord as both say Amen," Tonya said, hugging her again.

"That's it, that's all it took?" Melissa said slowly standing. She shook herself and a smile came over her face — her tears were happy now. "Wow, I feel like I just took off a hundred-pound backpack. Am I a Christian now?"

"Yes, you are God's child now," Tonya said happily.

Melissa reached out and grabbed Tonya and hugged her, and said, "Thanks! I got the change I wanted. I just don't feel the same anymore."

"That's it, you got it! My Dad's got a book called *Fresh Start*. It will help you grow as a Christian and he has a free Bible to go along with it for you. You are welcome to come to our church." Tonya said happily, "Let's go back into the house."

"Fine, thank you Jesus and thank you Tonya," Melissa said, smiling like she never had before.

Part IV

Chapter 28

Charleton had left the office early to go visit a friend he hadn't seen in a while. He figured he knew he needed to talk to someone in regard to his relationship with his wife. He wanted to go in on a positive note. Feeling like most men, a failure in this area would be the most devastating of all. The man he chose was Tonya's father, Reverend Edward Green. They had become friends when Tonya and his son, Ted, were dating three years ago. Charleton had deemed him too religious to be chums, but now he had some questions for him, as most people do when things aren't going right in their lives.

Charleton and Joe, his driver, went north on Providence, then right on Nifong Boulevard to gas up the limo. He was sitting in the backseat, thinking about all that had happened in the last few weeks. He cracked the window a bit to see how busy the filling station was with the University students having returned; the whole town was busier. He noticed the racing flags flickering overhead; red, yellow, orange and green. Displays of oil, windshield washer fluid and soda resting against the bottom half of the blonde brick building where the cashier was located. He watched Joe finish filling up and enter the store. There was a line so he figured it would take a bit.

Before he could finish, he saw a shiny black Cadillac STS pulled up directly in front of him and two thugs got out. Charleton knew exactly who they were — Jonesy's boys Sky and Razzy. Sky stood outside Charleton's window trying to discreetly show his switchblade — in the meantime, Razzy had gotten into the limo and shoved his 44-magnum in Charleton's ribs.

"Look, the boss sends you this message; you've got until noon on Friday to sign him as your partner or else! And if you don't know what the 'or else' means, at least Carl does, and I should say that …"

"Shut up bonehead! He don't need to know everything. Like he said, Charlie, by noon Friday. Jonesy's pretty ticked off at you. He ain't in a very good mood." Razzy said snarling at Charleton.

"Tell your boss I don't appreciate him sending his gorillas to talk to me. Noon, yeah! Tell him he's not getting half or even one percent of Magenta, Inc. not now, not ever! It would be over my dead body." Charleton said boldly as he glanced to see Joe returning after paying for the gas. The "gorillas" as he called them backed away quickly, but not before they punched Charleton in the ribs.

"12:00 noon Friday," Sky said through the window. "We'll be in touch." Sky and Razzy left just before Joe entered the car. Joe looked in his mirror to see Charleton still doubled over some as he heard a black car squeal off. He looked out the windshield. He knew exactly who it was.

"Boss, are you all right? Jonesy's boys again — we need to call the police."

"No — no I'm fine. Take me to the church. I'll be fine. I quit running from trouble a long time ago." Charleton said, nodding for Joe to drive to the church, which was about a mile away.

The parking lot of the large church was mostly empty except for the church secretary, associate pastors and the pastor's car. Each parked in spots accordingly.

Charleton had Joe park the limo in a visitor's parking area taking up four spaces — parking across them. Charleton got out and walked toward the tall building with four glass double doors — one saying 'Welcome' on it.

He entered the large foyer, empty except for a Bible tract table, a 'Welcome Visitor' sign in book, which was on a table hooked to the wall, and pictures of Jesus on the paneled wall — and a saying, 'Enter to Worship' above the doors leading into the main Sanctuary.

Charleton noticed the wooden doors to the main sanctuary were open. He saw no one inside. Instead, all he saw was a huge stage with large screens hanging down from both sides, a piano on the right, an organ on the left and a set of drums behind it, encased with Plexiglas.

Behind the pulpit was a huge wooden cross, it protruded out of the mosaic stones on the back wall resembling a cave, a stained-glass window with a Crucifix, a dove and a crown off to the side. Above the cross it simply said in huge letters, 'Jesus Saves'.

Charleton saw this and perhaps being drawn by all that he had experienced and heard lately, he went to the front of the church and looked around to see only a bunch of empty blue padded chairs. He continued looking around, wondering if someone was watching him.

He looked up again at the cross and the words 'Jesus Saves', and right where he stood, he knelt down. He didn't know why he was doing so, but he felt he needed to, like Carl, get things right between him and God. He fell on his knees and mumbled something only he and God understood, then he cried and cried and cried.

Chapter 29

The General had a dilemma on his hands. The media had already convicted Charleton of being an abusive husband, a tyrant, and an all-around awful person, to the point whether he was guilty or not it really didn't matter. The question now was, could any respectability be salvaged so that the general public could see another side of Charleton. This needed to be discussed. Maybe his philanthropy could resurrect a decent showing in the primary, if he ever made it that far, but even before that, next Monday morning Charlton was supposed to speak at a press conference to tell his side of the story and to formally announce his candidacy.

However, even above all this, the General had received some disturbing information about Charleton from a reporter and some photographs from his own staff that showed Charleton, again, was not being truthful with him.

The General, not being an irrational man, would at least give Charleton one last chance to explain himself with a visit to his home.

As Charleton entered looking a little haggard as if he had been on his knees, crying all day, he said, "Hi General, what's going on?"

"Charlie — Charlie boy, you look like you haven't slept for days," the General watched him sit down in a daze as if his mind was miles away.

"I'm fine, I really haven't been better. It feels good to work on some personal issues sometimes," Charleton said, feeling a change beginning to take place in his life.

"Something to drink?" the General offered as he sipped his coffee from a huge mug that read 'Magenta for Governor 2004'.

"Now, that's quite a mug — you must still have faith in me," Charleton said looking at his mug, the title Governor still sounded great.

"Yes, but give me reasons to keep the faith, Charlie. Do you remember Ms. Rose LeVon?"

"Yes, she's the best-looking reporter I've seen since Connie Chung."

"That's true — she is easy on the eyes and also, she's the most honest reporter I've seen in a long time. She came by and had a talk with me. She dropped over a hospital report along with your private physician's report. Not good! Why didn't you tell me all this before? I just don't understand this pattern of abuse, why weren't you thrown in jail! Was everybody so dense they didn't see you were obviously abusing Constance?"

Charleton leaned back, "You too! Are you on my case too? I'm not a monster! I'm not!" he exclaimed trying to convince him.

"Do you really think I can help you become Governor? Why I'll be laughed out of politics for good! If this leaks to the press you'll be a dead duck," the General said, not at all happy with Charlie, "and another thing, rumors are going around that you're connected with the mob now."

"Not true! Not true! Jonesy, that hoodlum from out east that came here a few years ago, he's trying to muscle himself into my company. I won't let it happen!" Charleton said with fire in his eyes.

"And these, explain these!" the General said, pushing a fat manila folder toward Charleton.

"What's this?" Charleton asked as he grasped the envelope.

"You'll see."

Charleton opened the metal tie, pulled back the flap, seeing it was full of photo's he poured them all out at once. He looked at them recognizing two people immediately, but not the third smaller person.

"Who do you see?" the General asked, leaning back in his chair, scratching his bald head, moving his red and white stocking cap around.

"My wife, Tonya and the child — he looks to be around two or three years old. It was taken at a park; I've never been there. If I have, it's been a while. I haven't seen Tonya in about three years, since my son and her broke up. I don't get the connection," Charleton said, looking obligingly at the photos, raising some up to get more light.

"That little one is your Grandson, yours, my sources say, Ted, your son, is the father and Tonya Green, Reverend Green's daughter is the mother, and they were never married. I thought you said you didn't have any more skeletons in your closet. I'm sure the press is trying to break this story too."

"No — no way. Ted couldn't be that stupid. A son and Constance — I wonder how long she has known about this and hasn't bothered to tell me. I'll — I'll …" Charleton said in a threatening tone.

"You'll what? You better not lay a hand on her again. Look, I'm this close," the General said, waving his hand in the air showing the "this close" sign with his fingers, then he continued, "I'm this close to dropping you all together. In public you came across to me as morally upright and whose family is in order, but I find that your personal life is a mess. It's hard for me to believe and yes, I do have a confession to make; I sent Rose LeVon to find out what you were really like. She's fresh out of Truman State, she finished first in her class, and she's started her own magazine — she's quite a lady. That's why she came to me first with her findings. The way you talked to her about women on your way to Sedalia, I believe, the other day — she was afraid of your attitude. She feels you don't like women for the right reasons. You use them to manipulate them for your own use. Women aren't sex objects, Charlie, they're people, human beings with feelings just like you and I, or have you forgotten that? Charlie, you have really disappointed me. I hate to be so blunt. You see, I felt like I was an Alfred E Smith of New York who urged F.D.R. to run in 1928. I was urging you because I felt you could really grow this state, grow the Midwest and maybe even reach the White House and change the whole country. Right now you have so many buzzards circling overhead it'll take a miracle to even get this campaign off the ground."

"By the way, there was no planted reporter — I just said that, so you'd keep on your toes. Evidently that didn't help, Monday at 10:00 am you're supposed to go before the press. I think you better go home and get your house in order first. Yes, I'm working behind the scenes leaking all the positive things you've done, but that may not be enough. Go home and have a long talk with your wife. If I were you, I'd get down on my hands and knees and beg her to forgive you and I'd talk to your son and find out why this happened, to have a kid out of wedlock, because that truly shows a lack of self-control. The only one clean is your daughter, Teresa. She evidently lives the way she should. You told me when you came in that, 'I still have faith in you.' Monday morning at 10:00 am we'll see if the public still does."

CHAPTER 30

It was around bedtime when Tonya finally relaxed. It had been a very busy day. But a very good one, especially in regard to Melissa, who became a Christian, but she felt sad for Constance whose life was made miserable by an abusive husband.

She prayed for both women, and she realized both were powerful, beautiful and charismatic in their own way, but they both needed peace.

Tonya talked to God about how Melissa was a bit intimidating at first but afterwards there seemed to be a genuine rapport between them and she prayed they would one day become good friends. Also, she let God know that she had given Melissa a *Fresh Start* book and new Bible, and she had also let her read the letter that Ted had sent through his mother Constance. She felt she should be totally open with Melissa.

Tonya realized that Melissa was so much calmer at the end of the visit than at the beginning. She had sat silently in Tonya's father's study and the only response she had said, "Ted could use Jesus too."

Melissa, Tonya noticed, left happy. She hugged her, Zelda and Pookie. She even kissed him on the cheek. Tonya knew indeed Melissa was a different woman.

Sitting alone in her massive bedroom in a red fabric overstuffed chair, next to a large walnut desk with a PC, TV, jewelry box and various awards she had received at school in writing, English literature, speech and shop class. She retrieved the letter from Ted. After having read it at least three times already she was still trying to discern his sincerity.

Dear Tonya,

I hope you are doing well? I'm sure you never wanted to hear from me again, but my mother told me that you had contacted her to let her know 'we' have a son. First, I ask you to forgive me for the way I treated you that night. I was just plain stupid! It took you and I both to produce that child, it wasn't just you. I should have been more understanding. I should have never said the things I said. You are not a dog, far from it. You are very much a lady and yes, I'm sure a lot of men would love to have you as their wife.

Also, I am so glad you didn't abort Pookie, as my mom says you call "our" son. He did not deserve that fate. I will understand if you do not wish to have a relationship with me, but I would like to have a relationship with Pookie.

I guess you heard about everything that has happened to my family. Good or bad, it has caused me to think about what is important in my life.

I always wanted a son and now I have one. I used to believe kids should be planned, they should come at a convenient time, but I know that isn't always the case. I said to you, 'I don't want no stinking kid,' how foolish of me. It's not the kid's fault he's here. So please forgive me for what I said and did that night.

Speaking of that night, I recall the night we first made love. I can't lie to you and say I didn't love you, because I did! You made me feel like a man should. Was it real love or just lust? Whatever it was, I'm convinced it was wrong. We both should have waited until we were man and wife. I really believe that would have been best.

I hope I'm not sounding too religious, but lately I've been praying and thinking a lot about what's wrong and what's right.

Honestly, I'm not sure where we go from here. I know I still need to do some more soul searching, but I really do want to be in our son's life.

About us, well I'm not sure how I should feel, or how I do feel, but I would like to meet with you both, maybe then things would become clearer.

I'm sorry I'm not a better writer, but I'm writing this at 3:00am because I couldn't sleep so I hope it's coherent enough.

Well — you take care, and I hope to see you both real soon.

Yours Sincerely,

Teddy R Magenta
Phone # 573.443.1944 cell

Tonya folded the letter and put it in the long top drawer of the desk. She leaned back in her overstuffed chair, still wondering if Ted was sincere.

The part of the letter where he said, "I recall the night we first made love, I can't lie to you and say I didn't love you …" This thought ran through her mind over and over like a horse galloping through the plains.

"Does he still love me? Does he still want to be with me? If not, what does he want from me?" All these questions invaded Tonya's mind making her thoughts still unclear, "but if he has any feelings for me, why didn't he mention his fiancée, Melissa? Surely if he loved her wouldn't it be easy to write, 'I have found another, but I do want a relationship with Pookie'. How come he is so vague on how he feels about me?"

Finally, Tonya shook her head trying to rid her mind of all these thoughts. Then she said softly to herself, "I can see why he chose Melissa; she is more beautiful than I am — her hair, her body, everything is better. No, I must stop thinking about all these things. My brain is gonna explode. Relax Tonya — relax." She stopped talking to herself and she finally got out of her chair and walked over to her bed which had already been pulled back like a turnover. That was where she had first put Pookie to sleep until she transferred him to his bed earlier.

She sighed as she gazed at him — then went down on her knees to the carpeted floor. She put her hands together in the prayer position like she had so many times as a child … she began to pray.

"Dear Lord Jesus, my mind is so busy — so full of the cares of this life. Please give me peace again, your peace that the world can't take away."

"First, I thank you today for my son. I know he doesn't understand why his father isn't around, but please tell his little heart how much I love him and how much you love him."

"Yes, I know Pookie did not come the way he should have, but he's here and I am so glad. He's brought me tremendous joy from a bad situation. I could not imagine living without him."

"Please, Lord, help me to understand my feelings for Ted. Give me the strength to be honest and sincere with him because I know my heart is sometimes easily swept away."

"Also watch over my sister Amber and my father and mother. Please watch over Constance who has to make a difficult decision which must be made. Please be with her husband Charleton, convict his heart and Lord never let him be mean to Constance again!"

"Be with Melissa and thanks for saving her. She really needed some answers in her life. Be with Ted and show him what a real father should be. I know I've said a lot. I know I've asked you for a lot, but I also know I serve a big God. Thank you for listening to me tonight, always being there for me but most of all thank you for loving me. Amen!"

CHAPTER 31

Ted had wondered, ever since he had given his letter to his mother to give to Tonya, what she thought about him. Not long after giving it to his mother he realized he hadn't proofread it, but alas, at 3:00 am his thoughts weren't clear at all, but at least he figured they were honest.

All day long he had debated whether to call Tonya or drive over to her house, but he reasoned to himself, "Not knowing how she feels about me could be very upsetting to both of us if I just showed up. Then again, I could look into her eyes and see what she really thinks about me."

Ted realized that these questions were not profitable because he didn't love Tonya anymore. Melissa was his woman now; besides he had rarely even thought of her in the last three years. Yes, he remembered her letters, phone calls and home visits but he had just wanted her out of his life.

Melissa wasn't clingy like Tonya. Melissa did her own thing then came back to him. He liked the fact that she didn't shadow him around, but he couldn't help but wonder that with the recent episodes of the last few nights, if there would even be a relationship with Melissa. Ted knew he dearly loved Melissa because he always said to himself, "she was quite simply the most beautiful woman he had ever met, and she came from good stock."

It was 8:30 pm and he was wondering when she would be home. She hadn't phoned which was unusual. He wondered briefly if something bad had happened to her, but he knew she could take care of herself. As he reasoned with himself, he heard her car drive up. He knew by the sound it was Melissa's Sebring convertible which was gold with a white landau roof.

He opened the door to greet her. He noticed under the garage lights that she somehow looked different. She had a new swagger to her walk.

"Hi babe — how are you?" Ted asked, kissing her on the cheek letting her cross the threshold, then he shut the heavy door behind her. He watched her put two books down; he recognized one as the Bible. He started to pick up the other book when she grabbed his arms and held them out.

"Guess what happened to me today?" Melissa said, smiling ear to ear.

"I don't know, you look different somehow, you actually look happy, which surprises me after the recent discussions we've had." Ted said, watching Melissa's face glow.

"I am different! I am happy! I went to see Tonya to talk to her about some things. She's nothing like you said. She's lovely, she's kind and just plain wonderful. The best part is she led me to the Savior. I'm a Christian now! Jesus came into my life! All my sins have been forgiven! It's great, isn't it?"

Ted smiled weakly not knowing what to say. He didn't run around in Christian circles. "That's great Baby, great, it's okay."

"Okay? Just okay! You should be a Christian — everybody should be a Christian. Jesus is so wonderful!" Melissa said, still smiling.

"Wow — you're really hyped. You saw Tonya, calm down, you're on cloud nine. Have you eaten anything? We can order pizza or something and snuggle on the couch. Then you can tell me about becoming a Christian and what you and Tonya talked about. Just relax." Ted said, sensing a real change in her as he tried to coax her into coming over to sit with him on the long sofa.

"Ted, no, it's not right anymore. I really can't stay with you. I'm a Christian now and we're not married, it's just not right. Sure, I don't understand everything, but I do know it's just not right." Melissa said, holding on to her Fresh Start book, as she moved away from him.

"C'mon, sit down, let's talk about this." Ted said, gently pushing her toward the couch, but she wouldn't allow it. He continued, "What? You're moving out? You don't want to live with me anymore?" Ted said, shocked at this, realizing she was truly a different woman.

"Yes, it's wrong."

"Huh? Wrong? Tell me about Tonya. I meant to tell you, I couldn't sleep the night you made me sleep on the couch, so I wrote her a letter. I knew my mother was planning to visit her, so I asked her to deliver it, sorry I didn't tell you sooner."

"It doesn't matter. I read it. She showed it to me." Melissa was too euphoric to be brought down.

"Oh, so what did you think about the letter? I know I should have told you." He said leaning back against the arm of the couch though he was still standing, he was unsure of what Melissa was going to do. She could be pretty feisty.

"It's evident you want a relationship with your son. I met him — he looks just like you — bushy eyebrows and all." Melissa said, rubbing Ted's eyebrows to show the resemblance.

"Really?" Ted asked standing up, "he looks just like me huh?"

"The spitting image. He's so cute Ted; I just want you to know I forgive you for lying to me. I don't understand what has happened to me at all. See these books I brought in? I'm sure they'll help explain everything. I still love you so very much, but on the way over here I just started to talk to God, that's what Tonya told me to do just talk to him like He is my best friend because He is now!"

"So much has happened to me lately, I think I need a little time to sort everything out. I haven't seen mom and dad in a long time. Maybe now would be a good time for me to go back East."

"Could I love little Theodore, or Pookie as Tonya calls him? I believe I could, matter of fact right now I know I could."

"Us, well, I just need some time to sort everything out. I'm not sure I really want to get married right now. I'm not trying to hurt you in any way, but I need you to give me some space, in time I'm sure God will make things clear."

Ted's jaw dropped. He tried to say something, but the words just wouldn't come. He thought about begging her to stay but he felt that would probably drive her further away. He was glad she wasn't angry toward him about writing the letter, however, he felt troubled that if she went home to visit her folks she might not come back. He thought, maybe she'll find another man.

He shook his head no, still not knowing how to respond, he just said, "sure — sure, whatever you think, Baby I love you too."

Ted reached over, hugged her and gave her a gentle kiss on her cheek, once more realizing for some odd reason that might very well be his last one.

Chapter 32

Constance had done what Tonya had suggested. She had called the local women's shelter and had gone for a visit. As she drove there, she imagined what she would see. Women — poor, uneducated and dirty with lots of kids by different fathers, but to her utter amazement she saw well-kept women, clean, highly intelligent; some were younger with kids from different dads, but one thing they had in common — they had all been abused.

She talked to a counselor named Lorreen, a heavy dark woman who didn't take anything from anybody. Lorreen's main concern was the welfare of women and children. She had also shared some statistics that had mortified Constance though she tried to shake them out of her head — one was that women were physically assaulted by an intimate partner averaging 6.9 times, according to the findings from the National Violence Against Women Survey, July 2000. Constance knew she had been beaten more times than that.

Would Charleton really be angry enough to kill her? She knew she really couldn't say no.

Constance admired Lorreen, who despite obviously dealing with the worst secret of society seemed cheerful and friendly but concerned.

Constance knew that everyone had seen her society write ups, but at the shelter they just treated her as one of them.

After talking a while with Lorreen, Constance arrived at the conclusion that right now was the very best time to leave her husband, but she felt she just wasn't ready, so she decided to go back to her estate, much to the chagrin of Lorreen, who advised strongly against it. Lorreen knew that sometimes, when a husband sees the woman leave with a suitcase in her hand, they become extremely violent. She tried to convince Lorreen that more time would allow her to be at peace with herself. Lorreen didn't agree but she left the decision up to her.

It was late Thursday afternoon when Constance, standing in front of her full-length closet mirror, took a good long look at herself. She smiled half-heartedly at what she didn't know. She looked around at the lavishness of her surroundings — all the gold, silver trinkets, fine artwork — some original — and the fine wall coverings and fabrics which she had picked out, and she reflected on how excited she had been when she purchased them, but now the excitement was gone. She would definitely trade them for five minutes of real joy as Tonya had explained to her.

She looked back into the mirror as if she wanted to become a part of it and said to herself, "I really can't stay here anymore. I deserve to be treated better. No one deserves to be beaten, no one," she thought to herself knowing these thoughts weren't original, but they were growing more important.

"Where shall I go? I really don't want to stay at the shelter. Tonya has offered me a room and Teresa asked me to stay down under, but that's just too far away," Constance thought. As she was still trying to reason with herself, she continued, "but Charleton, how will he make it without me? I pack all his suitcases for his trips. I color coordinate his clothes. Without me he'll look like — who knows what."

"I take care of the day to day here at home — everything will be chaos if I leave. I'm the one who makes sure Frances prepares his favorite meals, I plan the parties. Without me no one will have any direction, then again, maybe they'll do just fine without me. Like the old adage says, 'you won't miss the water until the well runs dry'. Boy, I hope Charleton gets the message."

Constance mixed all these thoughts around like a fine harvest stew when she finally opened the closet door to pull out her blue leather suitcase.

She opened the large one to find all the smaller ones inside, made of the same material. She removed the smaller ones and started to pack a few things. She pulled down a few of her pant suits — the one's she liked the most. She figured although she was unsure of her destination, she wanted to be comfortable.

Constance took down a few of her more elegant evening gowns, especially a black sparkling one which she had purchased on a trip to California to buy antiques. It was an old, restored gown that had been worn by Judy Garland, that's what the Boutique owner had told her. She bought it hoping deep down inside it might one day take her "over the rainbow." As she dropped it in front of her on the bed, there was a soft knock on the door, then a voice, "Mrs. M, may I come in?"

"Yes, come in Frances."

Frances entered quietly. When she saw Constance putting the Judy Garland dress in the suitcase, she hurried over to her and asked, "Are you really going to do it this time or are you just thinking about it?"

"Frances, I have to. I just can't take it anymore. If you hadn't been there the night he attacked me at the dining table, he might well have…" Constance said hesitating, not wanting to say the word. She turned and scooted her suitcase over and sat on the large bed, Frances sat down beside her.

"Kill you, is that it? I'm so glad you're leaving him. I came up here because you hadn't come down in a while. You were just so quiet. I know you've been going through a lot of things lately." Frances said smiling, as she always did when someone was hurting.

Frances always tried to cheer them up. She continued, "Mrs. M, if I may be so blunt, you don't deserve how you've been treated, you're a very good person. You've treated me great since I came here. You pay us well; we get time off when we need it, you give us a Christmas bonus. I just hate to see you like this. Why now? I really thought you should have left him years ago. Why now?"

Constance shook her head, then she looked at her suitcase, then at Frances and saw her deep brown eyes, surrounded by her soft dark skin making her look so comforting.

She said, "It's just a lot of things. One is I can no longer see a future with Charleton. I don't think he has a clue of how awful he has treated me. 'Sticks and stones may break my bones, but words will never hurt me' what I lie! Yes, sticks and stones can hurt you but it's the words, they stick in your heart like a dagger. Can you imagine when he came home five years ago this week, after sleeping with that woman, he came home and kissed me and he made love to me and he told me I was the only woman in his life, that he couldn't love another."

"The next morning, I found a cheap knock-off of Victoria's Secret negligee, an ugly green one. What I lie! I woke him up that morning and threw it in his face and do you think he confessed? No! He hemmed and hawed around saying it was just a mistake. That it was one of his partner's negligees that got packed in his suitcase by mistake! Ha! Lies! Just lies! He didn't confess the truth to me until the end of the day, after I kept hounding him. Frances, how could he hold me and love someone else?"

"I don't know. I just remember how angry you were — you two didn't speak for weeks. It sure was pins and needles around here. I had to walk on eggshells all the time." Frances said watching Constance's eyes flash with pain and sorrow, growing wet with tears.

"Yes, I'm sure it was."

"Where will you go? I'll miss you. Will you ever come back?" Frances asked with a yearning in her voice.

"I'm not sure. Teresa wants me to live with her, and other friends have offered me places to stay. I'm not sure about leaving, but I've got to do something. God knows how much I tried to be the good wife and do the right thing. I've really tried to live for him. I've tried to do everything his way, but I just can't do it anymore. I can't be a Stepford Wife." Constance paused briefly then continued, "I know all this makes me sound like a whiny kid, but I just can't continue to live like this. I was so frightened the day he attacked me. I genuinely was afraid for my life. No woman, me included, can or should live that way."

"It's funny how our pasts seem to haunt us, Frances, like a constant shadow. I don't want to die by my husband's hand, I don't," Constance said bursting into tears.

"Oh Mrs. M," Frances said instinctively, reaching over and hugging her warmly, "there, there, you're doing the right thing."

Frances started to cry also, hurting for her, not sure of her comment about her past haunting her. She thought now wasn't a good time to delve deeper. She cried too, because she knew she was losing a great friend.

After a few minutes Frances said softly, pulling away from the embrace, wiping the tears from her own face with a tissue from her smock, she gave one to Mrs. M. "You're sure welcome to stay with my family awhile. Sure, you won't live like you do here, but you'll be safe and I'm sure Charleton will never think of looking for you at my house."

"Thank you, you are so wonderful," Constance said, drying her eyes and leaning over to hug Frances, "maybe I will take you up on your offer. I guess I better finish packing. Since you're here, tell everyone they can go home early, I just don't want to deal with them asking me a lot of questions if they see my suitcase. You understand. Is supper ready?"

"In the process," Frances said as she got up when Constance resumed packing.

"Just put it in the oven to keep it warm and put a note on the refrigerator telling Charleton his supper is in there. I won't be staying to eat and, Frances, I do appreciate you so very much. I'll miss all the help you provide by keeping the house in order! Thank You! Well, I want to finish packing. Charleton gets home about 6:30, and it's after 5:00 now. I think it's best to leave before he gets home. I don't need another fight. I just want to live in peace."

Frances didn't say much, she just nodded that everything would be taken care of as she left the room.

Constance wiped her eyes once more and resumed packing.

Chapter 33

Charleton had left the General's home realizing his family was a mess. The General was not happy with the national and local news media's viewing of him as a wife beater who wanted to be Governor. The National Organization of Women (NOW) was after him. The local women's shelters were starting grassroots campaigns against him, local churches were not happy with him because he was destroying the sanctity of marriage and above all, that the General felt his son Ted had no self-control to produce a child out of wedlock.

Charleton had so many emotions swirling around in him like a sink full of water with the drain plug removed, swirling around and around. He felt better when he cried out to God at the altar earlier that day, and for a moment he felt cleaner and lighter, but by now he realized, instead of leaving everything at the altar, he had picked all his troubles back up and was starting to get angry again.

The idea of him not being Governor bugged him. He knew other than being on lots of boards, he did not have any political experience, but being industrious he could and would learn from the best. He knew he was very capable of reading and studying, and he would most certainly be a success in whatever endeavor he pursued, but now his legs seemed to have been cut out from under him, all because of an embarrassing display by his wife at the party of the year that was meant to honor him.

"It's her fault, dang woman. She never listens to me. I know what's best for her," Charleton said riding in the back of his limo headed back to his estate a little after 5:00. He was headed home early to discuss some things with Constance. He continued, "If she would just shut up and obey me everything would have been fine! No — who am I kidding, come on Charleton, that's the problem, you can't control her. She has a mind of her own. That's the problem."

Charleton never took Constance leaving him very seriously. He, like everyone, had heard her yelling just before she jumped through the plate glass window, "I've got to get away! I've got to get away!"

He didn't know what she really meant by that. She had threatened to leave him so many times before, and she had even gone so far as to pack her things, but he had always been able to console her — even after one of his beatings, but now something seemed different ever since the night the kids jumped on him about the way he treated their mother. Beyond that the whole world knew there were problems in their family, serious problems. He wondered if she would really stay or leave this time.

"Of course she'll stay. Without me she won't have a dime. She won't know how to do anything. I made her! No, shut-up, Charleton, she has her own checking account. She has money, friends and she really could make it without you. Maybe she has a lover, that's it! That's why she's acting so strange, but — whom? She flies all over the world for her antiques, but wait she's gone to LA three times last month! That's it! She's probably got a Hollywood hunk — No, no," Charleton mumbled to himself, realizing his mental gymnastics were wearing him out.

As he pulled up to the front of his estate, he saw the front door open and two figures standing in the doorway, one was Frances, her tall lean figure was unmistakable. The other was his well-dressed wife carrying a suitcase. He thought, "Maybe she was leaving on another antique hunting trip, but wait, I see only one suitcase, which she never carries. Where's the other limo? I only see her car. What's going on?"

Charleton rolled down the window to get a better look and noticed that both women saw his limo approach at the same time. They immediately headed off the porch and for Constance's Maserati Spyder. He noticed that Frances pulled out her cell phone as she ran.

"Stop the car, Joe! Stop here!" Charlton yelled at Joe as he slammed on the brakes right behind Constance's car. Charleton jumped out and ran over to Constance who had opened the driver door and tossed the suitcase in and was trying to get in herself. Charleton grabbed her arm stopping her from getting in her car. "What are you doing? Why are you running? Are you trying to get away from me?"

"Leave her alone! Don't touch her!" Frances yelled, trying to push herself between them. She continued, "I'll call 911!"

"Go ahead! I ain't talking to you anyway. I think you need to find another place to work!" speaking softer, "Babe, where are you going? Just tell me." Charleton pleaded, again grabbing his wife by the arm.

"I can't Charleton, let me go please, let go of my arm! If you have any love for me, you'll let me go! Please don't hurt me!" Constance cried bursting into tears.

He grabbed her tighter as he yelled, "You can't go! You can't! You're my wife, you can't go!" He grabbed her tighter and tighter, trying to pull her out of the car.

Joe, who always sat quietly in the car, but seeing this he got and ran to the tumult. Frances was grabbing Charleton, trying to make him let go of her. Joe ran up and shouted, "C'mon Sir, it ain't worth it, just let her go."

"Whose side are you on? C'mon you ain't going nowhere! Get off me Frances! Let go of me!" Charleton shouted using one arm to push her to the ground, where she scraped her knee on the concrete driveway. She immediately dialed 911.

"Please send the police to the Magenta mansion!" Frances said, breathless and angry, "Hurry! Please hurry!"

Charleton heard this and spun around, yelling, "Why you ungrateful…" He then kicked Frances in her chest, which caused him to lose his grip on Constance. That gave her just enough time to jump in her car and slam the door. When she started it up, Joe grabbed Charleton from behind and said, "Enough sir, let her go."

Constance, seeing her chance, floored the car, squealing the tires as she left. She, for some reason, looked into her rearview mirror and saw Charleton raise his fist in anger, yelling so loudly she could hear him inside her car. "Come back here! No one walks out on Charleton Magenta! No one! Constance, you're my woman! I own you! I made you! No other man would want you anyway!" Tears burst from her eyes. The scene from the day her mother was killed once again burned in front of her — allowing her to hardly notice the sirens in the distance.

CHAPTER 34

It was definitely embarrassing when Ted had gotten the call to bail his father out of jail for assaulting his wife and his maid. The cable networks had already picked up the story and were broadcasting it every hour.

Ted noticed his father didn't say much as they exited the police station downtown, covering his head from all the reporters outside with a small bag of his personal items. He just mumbled that his mother had left him, and they'd talk about it later.

He watched his father get into his limo and drive off. He shook his head realizing his father had never been in court other than for lawsuits of disgruntled employees — which were very few — or other business factions that just weren't happy with the way he did business, but now, to be arrested, to have been fingerprinted and having to take a mug-shot, his father the most powerful man in the Tri-State area, how hurt he felt. Ted really wished he could change his name right now. The Magenta name had a black mark on it, a big black mark!

When Ted arrived at his house, it was late, around 9:30 pm. He went upstairs and took a long hot shower. As he was toweling off, he looked out the open bathroom door at his bed, how empty it looked with Melissa gone. He knew he loved her, and though it had been a three-year love affair, he knew his dad, being married for 33 years, had to be so devastated to have his wife, Ted's mother, walk out on him.

Ted ran his hair dryer along the middle of his head making sure it was dry. He exited the bathroom and got into bed. He lay there with the only light coming from a beige lamp on a chrome and glass nightstand. He liked modern furniture. He looked on the nightstand at a photo taken just last summer where Melissa and he vacationed in Venice just twenty miles north of Nice. They stayed at The Chateau Domaine du St. Martin. Oh, how they feel in love all over again. It was during that time he had proposed, and she had accepted, but alas, as he laid there staring up at the vaulted ceiling he really wondered if Melissa was ever coming back.

She had only called once to let him know she had arrived at her parent's home in Sutherland, Virginia and that was it.

Melissa meant the world to him and her being gone left him feeling empty. He felt he needed a woman to be close to again.

Ted knew he had always loved women. He loved the way they walked, talked and smelled. He hated being alone. He wanted someone he could wrap his arms around, kiss on the neck and whisper sweet nothings in her ear.

Ted kept thinking that maybe Melissa was really gone for good. He knew overall he had treated her really well — even though once he had almost smacked her for getting a bit too chummy with a foreign yacht builder at the annual Fort Lauderdale International Boat Show, where she was a spokesmodel, even though she said the kiss on the cheek was completely innocent, CNN had picked it up as something more. However, after further discussion all was right with the world again.

Yes — Ted knew they had their occasional spats, mostly over other men that flirted with her whenever they were dancing. Like his mother, Melissa calmly let the men know that she had come with him and was going to leave with him. Melissa, Ted knew, was irresistible and such a stunning beauty. To wonder if she might not ever return to him agitated him all night. Yes, he was happy for her conversion to Christianity, even though he didn't understand everything that was happening to her. She looked so happy. He had to conclude that the change was real, and he wondered, with all the changes going on in his life and his parent's life, that seeking God may not be a bad idea.

Ted had tried to get his father to tell him where his mother had gone. He had just mumbled that he didn't want to talk about it and leave it at that.

No matter how he would lie on his bed, on his side, stomach or back, sleep would elude him. Thinking about his father's arrest, his mother's disappearance, his newfound son, his girl being gone and now the paparazzi being after him wherever he went, everything was spinning around in his mind like a Cuisinart blender.

Ted decided to take a deep breath and maybe by concentrating on his son — maybe he could start calming down. It worked some until he began to think about Tonya. Did he or did he not have feelings for her? After all, he did love her at one time, but now he had moved on from Tonya, who was cornbread to Melissa who was all croissants. He knew he couldn't honestly compare the two, but how could he forget Tonya's naïve smile. He relaxed a little after seeing it in front of him in his mind, but he wondered — could he really develop a relationship with little Teddy without developing the desire to build a relationship with Tonya? Ted knew he had never been good about developing friendships with women, where a love had once been, ever since he was in sixth grade. He had fallen in love with Peggy Martin, who later dumped him for a more, as she put it, fun loving guy. She had been the first girl he ever kissed on the lips and years later that still bothered him. He knew he wasn't a playboy, at least most of the time. He tossed and turned a little bit more, but finally he remained still — then a real peace came over him when he decided that maybe the best solution would be to just get ahold of Tonya and his son and just spend some time together. Yes, Ted knew three years was a long time not to be around each other. He thought, was the hatchet really buried, was the water truly under the bridge, or was the hatchet removed, and a new bridge built? He knew he had taken one step by writing Tonya. He thought what could he lose by taking a second chance?

Ted finally fell asleep.

CHAPTER 35

Since Tonya liked the water so much, when Ted and she talked, it was decided that they would meet at Easley, about ten miles south of Columbia, where the Missouri river flowed through. The water was always peaceful. It seemed to relax her since her dad and her skipped rocks together when she was old enough to skip them.

Easley was known for its tall shade trees, dirt beach and plenty of old tree trunks and stumps for sitting on. It was spectacular in the morning and resplendent in the evening because the different hues of the sun lit up the clouds like a rainbow being exploded by a fireworks display.

Pookie arrived in a blue Chevy SUV; Tonya saw Ted sitting on the edge of his silver and blue B.M.W. He was dressed casually in black trousers and a white beach shirt.

Tonya saw him wave to her and she waved back. She got out and went to the back seat to undue Pookie and didn't notice that while she was doing this Ted had come over to offer some assistance.

"Hi Tonya, do you need some help?" Ted asked, standing off to the side.

"No, I can get him, thanks. If you wish you can carry his bag with his food, juices and extra clothes," Tonya said, only quickly glancing at him as she leaned over to unbuckle Pookie from his white and blue car seat. "Here you go Pookie," Tonya continued as she reached down to the floorboard and picked up a plastic bag with a long shoulder strap. She handed the bag to Ted, who graciously accepted it.

"There he is! My he does look just like me. Hi partner." Ted said smiling, then making a goofy face at Pookie after he had made one at Ted.

"Say hi Pookie, this is your daddy," Tonya said, retrieving Pookie then putting him on one hip, "I guess I won't need my purse."

She pushed the automatic door lock button on her key ring then put the keys in the side pocket of the plastic bag Ted was now holding. She looked up at Ted, noticing that he was still so handsome. His body still looked muscular and fit and smelled so good. His hair was even combed just the way she liked it, parted on the right.

"You ready Ted? Let's go. There, that's a good spot." Tonya said pointing to a spot about fifty feet away where an old tree trunk made a great place to sit. "I'd better carry Pookie with those kids tossing that ball around over there; he'll run over and try to get it."

"A baseball player perhaps," Ted said softly. Thinking what all fathers seem to think, he'll be a sports hero.

"Perhaps."

As they walked, Tonya in the front, Ted just watched Pookie and played hide and seek with him as he peeked around his mother's shoulders.

"My — he's a handsome one."

"Yes, he is. It's so beautiful this time of day. Even a breeze is blowing. I know it's late August, but it looks like some of the trees are turning early. — Right here's fine." Tonya said, stopping at the tree trunk and sitting down, still holding on to Pookie who wanted to run toward the water.

"Whoa, in a minute — put the bag down there. Boy, it sure is lovely here. The river seems so peaceful."

"Yes," Ted said, watching Pookie 'running' in his mother's arms. He looked at Tonya, she had aged well, and she was even more beautiful than he remembered. Her fragrance captured him.

"Tonya, you're more…." Ted stopped, thinking perhaps it wouldn't be the best to say anything in that area right now. He continued with another train of thought, "I'm sure you heard about dad."

"Yes, it's all over the news — so sad, really. How's your mother? The news said the maid got hurt too," Tonya said, full of empathy as she pulled a toy out of the bag for Pookie to play — he was content for the moment.

"My mother — well, no one knows where she is, and Frances will recover. I know that sounds terrible, but I'm sort of glad mom left. I hope it will make dad wake up and smell the roses and …" Ted said being cut off by Tonya.

"Pookie, no, don't eat mud! — Yucky! Yucky! — Sorry to cut you off, go on," Tonya said, reaching in her son's mouth with her fingers and pulling a chunk of mud out, "sorry, go on."

"Well, some of those reports about dad's behavior are true, but look, I didn't come to talk about my parents, I came to talk about us. Hey Pookie, Pookie, say daddy, daddy," Ted said, bending down to his level and picking up a brightly colored ball with bells on it that Pookie had dropped, for a stick in the mud.

Pookie looked up at the strange man and made a face, then said "mommy", much to the chagrin of Ted. He stood up.

"Oh, he'll get used to me, it will take some time. Tonya, how have you been? Sorry I haven't kept up with your life at all," Ted said, feeling regretful.

"No problem now. Where's Melissa? I thought she might have come too. She really is a wonderful lady."

"Melissa left; she went back home to Virginia. She said she needed some time to think. I don't know what you did to turn her on to Jesus, but she's been on cloud nine ever since she came to visit you; this Jesus thing must be good for her," Ted said looking at

Pookie, then his mother, her hair, dark and straight, her face, round and full — her eyes, bubbly with a wisp of sparkle above them.

"Jesus is not a thing. He is a person. Everyone needs to have a relationship with Him." Tonya said boldly as she got up watching Pookie stare at a cardinal just a few yards away.

"Birdie, birdie," Pookie said pointing to a bush off to the left of him.

"Birdie, see the birdie?" Tonya said, watching the cardinal fluttering on a few branches then fly away.

"He really likes birds. Uh, well what did you think of my letter? Melissa said she read it too. I wrote it at 3:00 A.M. when I couldn't sleep."

"Yes, she did, and I thought you wrote it from your heart — pretty good for 3 in the morning. C'mon, let's walk toward The Wide Missouri. Our stuff will be fine here," Tonya said, stopping Ted from picking it up with a gesture of waving her arm.

"Well, I did my best," Ted said, reaching out to grab Pookie's hand with his free hand, the other his mother had.

"I like the part about you wanting a relationship with Pookie, that's great — I want that too, but when you talked about when we first made love that you did love me, I guess — you really did love me then. Everything is so unclear now. No-no, stay out of the water!" Tonya said, trying to grab her son, who had let go of both his parents to run to the water's edge, but Ted got him first.

"You little tyke!" Ted said playing with him — smashing his own face into Pookie's stomach, blowing air making funny noises, then he turned him around and put him on his shoulders, making Pookie chuckle.

Ted started to talk when Tonya, who was looking over the water at a few older men fishing, wearing their fishing caps with old lures hanging from them, looked straight at Ted and spoke, "I guess I just want to know, do you still have feelings for me? You really hurt me, Ted. I cried a lot of tears over that night; you know the one I'm talking about. I was angry for quite a while, some days were better than others, but I finally forgave you in my heart and I forgive you now in person. I don't hate you at all. I guess I just wish we'd have taken more time to talk things out. One day we're a happy couple, the next day you just disappear, and I don't see you for three years. The last thing I remember is seeing your taillights and me sitting in a big mud puddle with cold rain coming down. Ted, I really loved you. You were my whole life, but you left me — you just threw me away like an old pair of shoes. If it wasn't for God and my family, especially my dad, I don't know where I'd be. You see, Melissa felt the same way... I don't think you realize how much you hurt her. She believed in you like I did. Why did you lie to her about us being together? Were you embarrassed of me?" Tonya asked walking slowly back toward the tree trunk to sit down and get a cold drink.

"No. Well, I have no excuse really. I should have just told you the truth, I guess. Melissa was a once in a lifetime catch, I didn't want to lose her. I guess I wanted her to believe she was the first. I brought some tea, it's in my car," Ted said, removing Pookie from his shoulders and watching Tonya take a sippy cup full of some red juice, she drank a swallow to show Pookie it was good to drink.

"No, I'm fine — here Pookie come sit on mommy's lap," Tonya said to her son, as he came running over awkwardly as two-year-olds can.

Ted sat down beside her, but not too close. He sighed and said, "Tonya, I admit I treated you horribly, you have every right to ask me to leave and never be a part of your life. I hope you will believe me when I tell you I want to be there for Pookie. I'll pay any child support amount you want. I'll take him to the doctor if you can't. I will help in any way you need me too. You see, coming over here I really thought long and hard about my life, the direction it's going, my child, our child needs to be my priority. Tonya, I was so wrong to desert you. You didn't deserve to be treated that way. I won't ever desert you again!"

"How do I know that? What assurance do I have? I don't ever want to get hurt by you again. Ever!" Tonya said, her heart was just not convinced. She started to cry as her son slowly drifted off to sleep after drinking his juice.

"Ah, I guess my word doesn't mean much now. I keep seeing my mom and dad's marriage fall apart and Melissa leaving me. I'm wondering if it's a sign from above that I need to work on what's really important in my life." He said, standing up. He stretched and continued as he looked down at Tonya and Pookie, "Tonya, I don't know everything that's going on with me right now. I mean I know it sounds awful, but I was sort of glad when Melissa left. It bothered me deep down inside when she told me she'd become a Christian. Honestly, I had never seen her so happy. She was not the same woman who had been arguing with me the past few nights before. She had a sparkle in her eyes that wasn't there before." Ted paused, as if he was really thinking about what to say next, then he continued, "You know, lately I've been praying some, just gibberish I suppose but something's going on in my life and I don't understand it at all."

"You asked if I still have feelings for you, I just don't know. I can't lie; I'll always have a special feeling for you because you have that simple trusting nature. Do I love you still? Tonya, you are even more beautiful than I remember. Motherhood has put a twinkle in your eyes, and your countenance is glowing. How foolish I was when I said no man would ever want you. To be frank, after seeing you now, I'm surprised you're still single. I mean, I don't see any rings."

"No, you don't. I thought it best for me right now to take care of my son first. Here, put this cup back in his bag please. Can you also give me a disinfectant wipe so I can clean his face?"

"Certainly." Ted said, doing what she requested. He continued, "How do you feel about me? Would you like us to have a relationship or just remain parents?"

"Ted, to be honest, I'm still sorting things out. Look at him, our gorgeous son, you wanted me to get rid of him, and a woman just doesn't forget that! I admit however, when I first saw you leaning on your car my heart skipped a beat like it did the first day I saw you outside the Hollywood Eight Theater. Part of me wants to hold you and kiss you and make things like they were, but part of me wants to never see you again because of the hurt you put me through."

"Since this is our first meeting, maybe time will clear things up for both of us. Some say you never forget your first love, I believe that's true." Tonya said looking straight into his eyes, which seemed to be lost in reflection. It was as if he was really looking inside himself for the first time in his life.

CHAPTER 36

Danner heard the news just like everyone else. It had rippled through the entire company that Mr. Magenta had been arrested for assault. Some of the women had quit because the assault had been against a woman, making it worse…his very own wife.

It rained quite a bit during the night in that part of the county north of Palmyra, so the work for the day was called off with more storms expected around mid-day.

Danner arrived at Charleton's estate to find it full of cable news trucks, with their satellite dishes in the air. Local, national and international networks were all there. Reporters were stopping anybody and everybody that went in and out, asking people how they knew Charleton Magenta and what they thought of him. Cops were trying to keep the peace and only letting people in that Charleton wanted. The police would buzz the intercom at the gate because today the gates were closed. Danner was allowed to enter.

As he drove up to the front steps, parked his car and walked quickly up to the massive front doors, he could see the outline of Charleton in a lattice frame window with the curtains closed. He could only imagine the scrutiny Charleton had to be under right now.

As Danner reached the front doors it started to rain and thunder, lightning covered the area. Before he could reach the top step Charleton opened the door, "Come in, and hurry. Gee I hate the press. They really are a bunch of vultures."

"Sure seems like it today," Danner said, as he caught a glimpse of a brown van approaching the gate, but he thought nothing of it.

"How are you doing? Rough night huh?" Danner asked, following Charleton down the hallway as the intercom buzzer sounded again.

"Geez, what is it now? Oh, I fired all the help, a bunch of freeloaders anyway, so I have to answer my own door, how primitive." Charleton said, turning around and going back to the intercom by the front doors.

"Yes, what is it now?"

"A delivery for Mrs. Magenta, antiques bought downtown," a security guard at the front gate said.

"Fine, send them around back, I'll meet them there, geez," Charleton said mumbling, "That's really all I need right now more old junk in this house — c'mon Danner, let's help them unload the truck so they'll get out of here sooner. Geez, but I'm really glad you came over. You seem like you're the only real friend I have right now."

"I'm glad to be your friend sir," Danner said, smiling at his boss.

Danner watched Charleton walk down the hallway. He seemed tired, alone and empty. He was dressed in the same clothes he woke up in though it was near noon, it was obvious. His hair was disheveled, his beard was stubby, his breath didn't smell too bad, but it wasn't good.

"I tell you Danner, the whole world seems like they're against me now. I mean, haven't I done good in this town? I've built roads and brought industry here and I raised the tax base. What do I get for all my good? I get arrested, that's all, because of an overly excited maid and a wife who decides I'm not good enough for her anymore and now the whole world thinks I'm a jerk," Charleton said, popping his lips, not believing all the misery he was going through. He continued, "It's like throwing rocks at a man in a glass house. Am I the only sinner in town? Give me a break!"

"You're being awfully hard on yourself sir," Danner said as he looked beyond the large glass patio doors, which led to the rear of the estate and the six-car garage. He then watched the brown van start to back-up in a rather unprofessional way. He jumped in front of Charleton; just as some more thunder and lightning flashed so fierce it rattled the windows.

"Sir, something is wrong. Their …" Danner said, being interrupted by Charleton, whose eyes suddenly grew bigger. As the van got closer to the patio doors, he yelled, "What — wait! That van is backing too fa…"

"Sir…!" Danner yelled as the van shattered the patio doors, coming inside the house. The back door of the van opened to reveal an old man pointing a double barrel shotgun at Charleton, while two young hoodlums, Razzy and Sky, jumped out of the van's front doors and ran toward the back of the van, both carrying AK-47s.

"OK, Charlie, Charlie, it's twelve noon! It's D-Day!" the old man said, pointing his shotgun at Charleton's head — the other two covered Danner.

"D-Day — you're really something Jonesy — you're really something." Charleton said still not afraid of him.

"Charlie, ol' Charlie, still trying to play the righteous card, what an idiot, it looks to me like you have no choice." Jonesy said, reaching carefully into his side pocket on his suit coat and withdrawing some paperwork. Then he thrust it at Charleton, "Sign this! Here, sign this! Then I'll just leave and go home, and I won't have any reason to splatter your brains all over your pretty marble floor."

"Okay, okay, you win." Charleton took the papers from Jonesy who, for a moment, removed the shotgun from his head. Charleton reached inside of his jacket for a pen. He motioned for

Danner to come over so he could write using Danner's back as a chalkboard.

Danner was shocked that Charleton gave in so easily.

Charleton just let out a sigh and scribbled something on it, and then he turned around and gave the papers back to Jonesy. As Jonesy received the papers he said to his henchmen, Razzy and Sky, "Maybe ol' Charlie isn't so bad after all. I mean, we're partners and I'm worth five billion dollars now and all is well with the…" Jonesy paused as he started to read where Charleton had signed his name, but Jonesy blew up as he read the words. "You're nothing but a jerk," he yelled at Charleton. "You're playing with me!" Just then Jonesy pointed the shotgun back at his head and started to fire, Charleton ducked and lunged for Jonesy. Danner, seeing his boss act boldly, jumped toward Razzy and Sky. This caused them to stumble back firing their AK-47's all through the Great Room, hallway, ceilings and floors, shattering vases, chandeliers and splitting upholstery. They all heard sirens heading for them, which they figured must have been triggered by the gunfire.

"C'mon, let's get out of here boss! The fuzz is on their way!" Sky yelled as he broke free from Danner, who was holding his own with him and Razzy.

"You! You!" Jonesy shouted, grabbing an AK-47 from Sky. He then pointed it toward Charleton and began to fire. Danner jumped in front of Charleton taking the bullets for him.

"Man, I can't even kill him!" Jonesy yelled, closing the back doors of the van. "I'm not done with you yet! You haven't heard the last of me…"

Charleton heard the van squeal off, throwing broken glass, wood framing and doorknobs everywhere. He ran over to Danner whose whole mid-section was a bloody mess.

"Danner, hold on son!" Charleton blurted out as he slumped to the floor, seeing all the blood and ripped flesh. All he could do was hold Danner close to him. He was like his own son and his blood was now soaking him. All he could say mumbling and crying was, "Hang on! Hang on! God, please let him live!" he begged. "It's all my fault! I should be the one suffering! Not him! Oh God, Oh God, please don't let him die!"

PART V
CHAPTER 37

Constance heard the news about the shooting at her estate from Frances. She stayed with Frances after she arrived home from the hospital with a skinned knee and bruises on her arms and face. Constance told her she was paying all of Frances' medical expenses and repeated often how grateful she was that Frances had risked her life to save her own.

Constance knew she really wanted to return home to find out the details of what happened, but quickly reconsidered, thinking the next time she would leave her husband he might kill her. She called her son Ted to find out how her husband was. She was relieved to find out he was safe but found out Danner was barely alive and on life support, having taken the bullets that were meant for her husband. All of this information tore her up inside because she did still love her husband. However, she was now more afraid of him than ever. She was also relieved that Jonesy and his cohorts had been captured attempting to escape through the rear of the estate.

She enjoyed staying with Frances, even though she thought her home was quite busy with four kids ages eight to fourteen and a husband. That left the only time to think late after the house was quiet. She would then sit alone in the kitchen, sipping green tea and wondering how her relationship had gotten so bad between her and her husband. Sure, they had their ups and downs as all couples do, but they always seemed to work through them. After the tirades and diatribes, they would come back together and be happy again. At least for a while but this time things were different. There seemed to be a real hatred between them. It was more than a general dislike that couples go through as they grow apart. No — this time there was a real gulf between them. This time she was really hurt. It wasn't just a slap in the face. This time it was as if there was a gushing wound like someone had been slicing her arm with a chainsaw.

The kitchen was rather small in Frances' modest home. There were colored drawings of horses, cats and flowers covering her refrigerator. Near the door that led outside there was a bulletin board with notes pin-cushioned on it. The walls were lined with pictures and paintings. On the countertops were cookie flour and sugar containers, all decorated with roosters, which Frances loved but for some reason never told anyone. Even the salt and pepper shakers were shaped like roosters. The kitchen was clean and well-kept with everything in its place. Constance sat quietly in a soft lavender robe and slippers, both monogrammed, with her hair all combed down making her look younger than she really was. She was there just to think, she turned on the light above the table, so she wasn't a distraction. She saw the rooster clock, just to the right of the bulletin board. It said 10:30. The house was so quiet; she could hear the ticking of the clock. She sat motionless, listening to each tick, which made her feel that her life was just ticking away.

Constance tried to imagine sitting in her wood kitchen chair with a rooster cushion, could she really make it without Charleton? Could she become her own woman again? She knew somehow in the last thirty years, being a mother, socialite and wife was where she was at. Constance had a life full of laughter and love that had been swallowed up by taking responsibility for someone else.

Constance recalled how she hated driving down the highway and seeing an older couple. The man driving, and the woman wearing a cloche hat staring aimlessly out the car window, counting her life down with each fence post with her husband chatting away about his great accomplishments. She knew she didn't want to end up like that. She wanted to do something with her life. According to her inner thoughts, she was tired of being just a Barbie doll or the bride atop a seven-tiered wedding cake. Nice to look at but when the wedding is over who cares.

"What if Charleton had died that night at the house?" Constance thought to herself, "what if the last memories I had of him yelling horrible things at me. Oh, that's not all Charleton was."

She shook her head and tried to recall good times. Like when they were first married and things were so wonderful, the lovemaking, the talk of dreams both small and great or their first anniversary. Unbeknownst to her, Charleton had put a little money back so they could rent a small cabin in Wisconsin in the fall of that year. They had walked down to the lake, a slight chill was in the air, fog rolled peacefully across the water as they sat on the shore. They listened to the sounds of the crickets, frogs and even some fish splashing in the water. They watched the sun slowly go down casting a magenta-colored glow on the rather peaceful surroundings. The view was simply beautiful, especially with the leaves turning.

She remembered how they went back to the small rustic cabin, and she knew Charleton really wanted to be intimate with her, but she lay on the bed and said softly "Would it be alright if you just hold me and wrap your arms around me and tell me that you love me? Tell me that I am your whole world. Please, Charleton, tell me that I am your whole world!" And as she thought of that defining moment in their relationship, she recalled that's just what he did. She knew in that moment that he really, really loved her. Oh, how she longed to return to that simple, awesome moment that made her feel loved, wanted, and safe. She wondered if it was possible to ever get that feeling back.

It was 11:30 pm before she collected her thoughts enough to go upstairs to the small bedroom she was staying in. It was adorned with stuffed toys, Barbie dolls and a ballerina lamp for Frances' eight-year-old daughter, who now slept in her mom's room while Constance resided in their home. The three sons were just across the hall.

She took her robe and slippers off, knelt by the bed and prayed softly, only wanting the lord to hear her. Soon she drifted off to sleep wondering what tomorrow would bring.

Chapter 38

The next morning Constance was awakened by a host of commotion upstairs and downstairs as well as outside the house. She rolled over and looked out through the frilled curtain to see people walking outside pointing at Frances home. Her heart dropped. She figured nosy neighbors had found out she was staying there. She knew it was time for her to leave. Dressing quickly and thanking her hosts, she left with some regret. She drove around until she found a small obscure motel in a town twenty-five miles northeast of where she was. A place where she felt she could just relax and reflect on all that had happened to her in the last few months.

After registering in her maiden name and paying cash, she went to her room to find it acceptable; it wasn't what she was used to, though it was the deluxe suite. Everything was clean but all the furniture was an old dingy brown. She figured it would work since all she truly needed was time to think.

She placed her suitcase on the only chair in the room and sat on the edge of the flappy bed, wondering what to do about her life — everything seemed to be such a mess. She had heard about the horrors that happened at her estate, it was all over the news. She tried to break her train of thought by turning on the TV, which was the only new object in the room.

She reached for the remote which was on top of the TV. She looked at it for a moment then turned it on top see a BowFLex commercial. Then she flipped the station again to see a Fox network doing a local story, and it caught her eye because it was about her husband Charleton. The reporter, with white hair and thin lips, was explaining, "Yes, he will talk to the press Monday at 10:00 am at his office on Lake Providence Rd. Yes, the billionaire Charleton Magenta will speak on his run for Governor in 2004. As you know, he was arrested after allegedly assaulting his wife and their maid Friday evening. I might add he has been accused of spousal abuse before; however, no formal charges have ever been made." Constance sighed, then she continued to watch and listen.

"In this photo you see them at a republican fundraiser for now President George W. Bush held in St. Louis. They really make a handsome couple. Political pundits are saying if Charleton Magenta runs for governor right now, it would be political suicide after everything that has happened in his personal life."

"It was just two weeks ago at his big kick-off extravaganza held at his lavish Southwood Hills Estate here in Columbia, Missouri that his beautiful, many say unstable, wife ran and jumped through a plate glass window, yelling, and I quote, "I have to get away! I have to get away!" Unquote. "'Where' is the question on everyone's minds. No one knows where she is, but rumors are surfacing that she may be staying with her head domestic, who was also attacked along with Mrs. Magenta when just two days ago, Mrs. Magenta was attempting to leave her husband, when he came home early and he reportedly flew into a blind rage — pushing his maid down, causing injury and attempting to extract his wife with force from her car. She was able to escape."

"In light of this Mr. Magenta still insists on running for governor of the state of Missouri and he will hold a press conference on Monday morning at 10:00 am at Magenta Inc.'s World Headquarters, he will…"

Constance turned off the TV not wanting to hear any more about the governor's race or the reporters calling her mentally unstable. She moved from the edge of the bed near the TV to the headboard, next to it a small nightstand with a lamp that had a paper-thin lamp shade showing a very dim bulb.

Constance spoke out loud, "mentally unstable? Me? What in the world do they think my husband is?"

She shook her head, she was not a woman without anxiety, but she was far from a basket case, she figured there were just a lot of things going on within her life right now.

The longer she sat there the more she realized that she really had left her husband. A thought that slowly grew more real inside her. She was finally free from him and this thought, she figured. should make her happy, as long as he never discovered where she was. She felt for now that she didn't have to worry about being hurt by him again, physically or emotionally. That thought at least for the moment comforted her, but the idea of her marriage breaking up made her very sad.

"Why do I despise him so much? He truly was the love of my life and now I shudder at the very thought of him. Is there no answer to all of this?" Constance said to herself out loud, sighing heavily. She then got up, crossing over to the only window in the room. There were two large sliding windows with an air conditioner with a heater below. The dark red curtains matched the bedspread and were opened since she entered.

She watched the traffic on Highway 54 moving along, oblivious to her pain. She stared at a white limo that looked like her husband's, but it didn't have the Magenta logo on the side in big blue letters.

She looked at a strip mall which had a Dairy Queen, dress shop, shoe store and a grocery store in it. Since it was Saturday, the whole place was busy. She was glad she had been able to check in before the crowds came and somebody recognized her, even though she did wear her hair down to try and cover her face.

As Constance watched families get out of SUVs, Mini-vans or cars, some seemingly happy: a mother, father, sister and brother all laughing, all really enjoying one another and she thought, "Why can't I have that? Why can't I just have a happy marriage? Why can't I have a husband that loves me and only me?"

She just stared and thought about where she should go from here. She didn't want to go back to Charleton. She didn't want to go half-way around the world to Australia, though it had been over a year since she had visited there. Her only excuse for not visiting more often is that she hated those barking and frilled lizards, but she wouldn't totally rule it out. Constance knew her husband would look for her there first, and right now she did not want to be found.

"Where is that place over the rainbow? Where is my Emerald City? I just want to go to a place where I can be loved and be happy." Constance said tearfully to herself, as she shut the curtains and returned to the edge of the bed.

She turned on the TV again, pushing through some more channels, ESPN, TV Land and the Travel Channel where she paused to hear a lady in soft clothing describe a resort in Thailand, Southeast Asia, called the Chiva-Som International Resort. It had a great atmosphere where a person could relax and be themselves, which is what Constance needed right now more than anything. She was desperate for it.

Having that settled, at least for the moment, she laid back on the bed and looked at the white pointed ceiling and the name 'Chiva — Som Gaveb if Kufem' came into her mind again.

"Haven of Life, that sounds so peaceful. I need a place of peace and quiet. It would be nice to stick my toes in fresh clean water, and what did Tonya tell me? Oh, what did she call it!? I believe it was Cor-Cor something. Cor Inquietum that's it, that restlessness in my heart that drives me to search for what is true in my life of love. Yes, it was something like that. It's a hunger I have deep within my heart. What can satisfy that? There has to be an answer. I can't go on feeling this need inside me. My heart aches and aches, but if maybe I go to Chiva — Som, maybe I'll find peace, but no! Why can't I have it now? There's got to be an answer." Constance said, rolling over on her stomach. She began to cry and yell out "God I am so tired of being miserable! I am so tired of being mistreated! I'm so tired of everything. I need some answers to my life. I can't keep just waiting! I need you! I need you now! God where are you? If you are real, show me! I want to hear from you now!"

Constance cried seemingly for hours, but when she stopped, it had only been an hour; she glanced up at the desk clock on the nightstand beside the telephone. It sure felt longer than that. She felt like she had cried all night.

Constance didn't know why, but she had been in enough hotel and motel rooms over the years that she knew there was usually a Bible in the nightstand drawer. She got up and went to open the drawer and there it was in brown leather, the Holy Bible provided by the Gideons.

She sat on the bed as she looked at it, not sure where to turn. Once more she said, "God, I need you! Where are you? If you are real, show me!"

Constance opened the Bible, thumbed through it and stopped at a specific place, though she didn't understand why, but she started to read at Luke, Chapter 6 verse 20 and 21, "and he lifted his eyes on his disciples and said, 'Blessed be the poor, for yours is the kingdom of God. Blessed are ye that hunger now, for ye shall be filled. Blessed are ye that weep now for ye shall laugh…'."

Constance's eyes grew big as she really seemed to absorb the words she had just read. She said out loud, "Thank you for hearing me, Lord. I want you to fill me with your goodness. Fill me with your presence. Yes, I have made a mess of things. Yes, I have tried to live without you. Please forgive me for pushing you out of my life. It's not about me, is it Lord? No, it's all about you!

Make me new, Lord, right now. I can't wait until tomorrow. Give me a new heart and let me have love for my husband instead of hate," Constance cried and sobbed and confessed all of her sins realizing she finally had a heart to talk to her Savior.

Chapter 39

All day Charleton refused to answer his home phone or his cell phone. He had made up his mind he did not want to talk with anyone. Reporters, satellite trucks and protesters clung to his front gate. He had declined to hire private security to watch the outside of his estate while the local police finished their investigation, amid broken glass, shattered chandeliers, ripped up paintings and scarred walls. Yellow police tape was everywhere. The only thing Charleton had done was call someone to board up the shattered patio doors. Charleton had decided he was so totally stressed out that he just sat quietly in his study, thinking about everything that he had gone through in the last few days and which hurt the most. He knew without a doubt, it was his wife leaving him. He really thought he still wasn't a monster. He reflected on the situation by saying, "I just had a bad day, Constance. She'll be back."

He sighed and rubbed his forehead with his hands. He thought about fixing a drink and figured his drinking would not add a thing to solving his troubles. Then he thought about Danner. The noble young man who took the bullets meant for him, he knew he was still recovering, but barely. He had come through the surgery to stop the massive bleeding. He couldn't help but think it should have been him with his chest ripped open.

Charleton stopped his thoughts for a moment, he thought of himself lying on the operating table, near death, being kept alive only by machines and a prayer. Was he really ready to die? Was he really ready to leave this world knowing the love of his life absolutely hated him right now?

"Hate," he thought, "What a very strong word. Surely Constance, my babe, doesn't really hate me. It's all a big misunderstanding. She'll be back. She can't make it without me."

Charleton stopped talking to himself when he heard the scurrying of the police in the hallway. He looked out his study toward the back of the estate to see his wife's beautiful flower garden ruined by Jonesy's getaway and the police in pursuit. He could see the ruts that were left in the soft dirt. He sighed and said quietly to himself, "Boy — she put a lot of work into that garden. Those tire tracks — it almost looks like someone stomped on every single flower. Oh, how she loved her roses. I wonder if her flowers will ever bloom again. Will her roses burst with color next year?"

Then, without warning, he burst into tears and cried out, this time not caring about the police, "Constance, I'm sorry! So sorry! Please come back! I need you! I'm a wreck without you, please come back!"

Chapter 40

Charleton cried for what seemed like hours but really, it was just a few minutes. He managed to gather his wits and head upstairs for a shower, shave and to dress. He combed his hair and came back downstairs to his study after talking with the police and investigators, who were just getting ready to depart. Charleton was trying to improve his mood. He was ready to at least have some peace around his home, even though in his mind there was none. Charleton made it over to his large button tufted leather office chair. He leaned back and tried to relax. He smiled briefly at all his paintings and portraits of tall ships, especially his favorite Stad Amsterdam, of which he had taken a copy to his board of directors on the east coast a few years ago.

He also admired his collection of books. He had all types of books from novels to construction to history, which were all stacked floor to ceiling with a ladder that rolled sideways in front of the shelves. He had read most of the books filling his head with so much knowledge that he mumbled to himself, "Maybe I could win on a game show. What good does it do for me to be head smart but not heart smart and lose my own wife! Constance, oh Constance. Babe, where are you?"

Charleton had already called everyone he thought might have an inkling of where she might be. His daughter Teresa said her mom wasn't at her house but that her church would continue to pray that wherever she was she would be safe. This did not console him at all because he couldn't stop thinking she has got to be somewhere. She didn't just fall off the face of the earth.

Finally, after his mind stopped spinning like a Ferris wheel, he managed to drag himself to the kitchen for some dry toast and a glass of skim milk. He had been ignoring the phone all morning, but this time he glanced at the caller ID and decided he might as well answer it. It was the General who Charleton figured would be even more irritated with him due to the recent developments. Oh boy was he ever! The General yelled so much and so loud that Charleton had to pull the phone away from his right ear, which really didn't help much. He could still hear the General, who had in no uncertain terms told him he would no longer support Charleton. He would however be at the press conference because, as the General put it, he was at least willing to go down with the ship. Charleton mostly just nodded to all of this, then said goodbye with a sigh. He was finally realizing that deep down inside he wasn't totally innocent of everything that had happened. He figured everything had just collapsed on him all at once, like a tidal wave causing a great ship to capsize. He personally felt like he was being thrown overboard.

Charleton made his way to the family room, which was virtually untouched. The room held the white baby grand piano, which Teresa liked to play since she was five years old. It also housed the fine sculptures, white leather couches and an overstuffed chair, a huge ten-foot marble fireplace with a life size painting of his wife. She was dressed like a royal queen wearing a bustle, a stomacher, heavy lace and a woman's headdress made of lace and linen with lapels. She truly looked like the queen of queens.

He stared at her portrait. His heart yearned for her. Finally, he sat at the piano. He tickled the ivories a little, playing chopsticks. He got up and walked around just trying to settle himself down. He looked toward the main gate to see the extra security he had finally decided to hire because he was trying to keep the peace with the protesters who weren't happy with his treatment of women. He just didn't understand it. He said to himself, "One bad day. I guess I shouldn't have pushed Frances. Yes, I shouldn't have yelled at my wife. I should have done this or that, but I did this instead, my old football coach used to say, 'if it's and buts were candy and nuts'."

Charleton just sighed heavily; wishing this whole day, this whole month was over. The intercom buzzed. He answered on the wall behind the piano, "Yes who is it now?" he said in a regretful tone, really not in the mood to talk to anyone still. "It's your son. He really wants to see you."

Charleton responded, "Yea, sure, let him in." He was not feeling the best about any of his relationships now, though he did know his son loved him. He added, "Tell Ted I'll be in the family room."

"Yes, certainly Mr. Magenta."

Charleton went back to the piano and waited quietly, peering out the large open French doors that led to the hallway, which was still a mess. It didn't take long for his son to enter with a soft smile, because he was genuinely glad to see his father. When he saw all the broken vases, chandeliers, bullet holes and yellow police tape, he declared, "Wow dad, what a mess!"

"Yes, be careful son, there's a lot of broken glass, watch your step. The cleanup crew and insurance adjusters will be here tomorrow." Charleton said, motioning for his son to enter the family room. He did, and Charleton stood up and hugged his son weakly, then said while sitting back down, "What brings you here son? My friends are getting to be fewer and fewer."

"Dad, quit saying that, you have a lot of friends. I'm sure they just don't understand everything that's happening right now, that's all. You know I really do owe you an explanation about, well, I'm sure you already know. I'm sure if you've been watching the networks, well I visited Tonya today and met my so…"

"Sorry to cut you off, I already know you have a son out of wedlock." Charleton said, interrupting his son.

"You're not angry?" Ted asked, pursing his lips in surprise.

"Son, the General told me. Does it really matter now with everything else going on? Getting mad with you just wouldn't help at all. I would have liked for you to have told me yourself though. I guess I've been doing a lot of thinking lately, especially about relationships. No doubt what you did was wrong, but nothing matters right now but me getting your mother back." Charleton said, his eyes watering.

"You really love mom don't you dad?"

"With all my heart! She was and is my only love. Yes, I messed up once again. Liquor can do that to you, but she is all I've thought of day and night for the last 33 years, honest." Charlton said becoming lost in the reflection of his love for Constance.

"Does she know that? Did you tell her that?" Ted asked. He knew growing up with his dad he never heard him ever tell his mom that he loved her, at least not in front of his sister or him.

"Well, I guess, I mean does a guy have to tell his wife every day, all the time? I mean I built her a mansion. I made sure she had her own airplane and that she wore Cartier watches, gold rings by H. Stern. She always flew out to have her hair done by Roberto CiCula. I made sure she was able to purchase a car with just her signature. She had everything she ever wanted. She was well cared for, so why do I need to tell her I love her? It seems redundant to me." Charleton said smugly, watching his son wiggle as he leaned over the piano, with its top open and slanted to the side.

"Dad, I know this might hurt when I say this, but I'm glad mom left you. You really weren't very nice to her sometimes and remember what I said, 'if you ever touched her again, you'd never hear from me again,' well I'm here to let you know I'm this close to doing that right now! I love you dad, but I love mom too. Women deserve to be treated better. As I was saying before you cut me off, I visited Tonya and got to meet my son, your grandson for the first time. He's a wonderful boy. Yes, I messed up, I should have married Tonya first, but the kid is here, and we all have to deal with him."

"You see dad, I made a big mistake by pushing Tonya out of my life, all because she got pregnant with my son. I missed out on so much by breaking our relationship off. I missed his delivery, his first birthday, first step, second birthday all because I was selfish. I wanted what was best for Ted. I was foolish. I wanted my career. I wanted to establish my own desire to be an attorney. If I had to do it all over again, I'd love the woman that I had my child with," Ted said boldly, watching his father hang onto every word. "Dad, I held little Pookie, that's what Tonya calls him. I looked at this little boy, this precious little boy, with 10 fingers like me, with toes like me and bushy eyebrows like me. To think, my God, I wanted Tonya to abort him. How could I have been so stupid?"

"Somehow looking at him and looking at Tonya, I finally realized what's important in life. It's not degrees. It's not building 401K's or having precious metals in your portfolio. It's having someone to love you and for you to love them. I looked into Tonya's eyes, and I saw joy, peace, and the knowledge that she's got her life right with God."

"She had every right to nail me to the wall for what I said and did to her that night, all because she was pregnant. Dad, I kicked her out of my car in a rainstorm, into the mud, on a dark road all because I wanted what was best for me!"

"I tried to move on with Melissa, but I knew deep down inside I really couldn't because my heart was still beating for the woman I left behind."

"Dad, I have been a fool with my life. It's time I really grow up. Love, sure, I don't understand everything about it, but it just seems to me it means to not put yourself before others."

"I know I've rambled a lot I'm sure, and I'm not trying to tell you how to live. But maybe if you would have told mom more often that you loved her and maybe if you held her more, rather than just yelling at her and smacking her around, she'd be with you now. Maybe none of this would have happened, the window incident, the assault, none of it."

"Dad, I promise you, if you ever touch her again, I will pull myself away from you. I realize today you don't seem to be in any condition to handle that today. I'll be at the press conference tomorrow, if you don't apologize to mom, Frances, to all the people you've hurt, including the citizens of Missouri, I won't be able to continue to support you. I know she's your wife, but she's my mother and I won't let any man lay a hand on her again, even you, dad." Ted declared with great conviction, realizing he had to take a stand.

Charleton looked at his son who had developed a fire in his eyes. He knew he had never spoken to him that way before. He stood up, rubbed his forehead with his left hand and said, "Son, you're right, everything you said was right. I don't want to be like this anymore. I really don't! Oh, how I miss my Constance. Babe, come back, please come back, please!" he began to sob heavily. His son knelt beside him, embracing him, trying to comfort his weary soul.

Chapter 41

It was a bright and sunny September day as Charleton stood in front of the podium outside the front doors of his World Headquarters building. The gold tinted windows reflected the brightness of the day.

The circle drive was full of radio and TV vans, local and network trucks with their antennas and satellites focused. Cars with TV logos and limos of other dignitaries as well as various officials from state and local governments made up the vehicles crowding the circle driveway.

Police, fully dressed and with helmets, kept order as a group of mostly female and a few male protesters walked round and round the Atlas statue in the huge water fountain. They had picket signs saying, 'Wife Beaters Don't Make Good Governors!' One said, 'Wife Beaters Don't Make Good Husbands Either!'

The press had their cameras rolling and long microphones that reached almost to Charleton's face. Charleton had dressed in his finest French cut suit which seemed to be all coordinated. His hair greased and combed. He was clean shaven and had used his best cologne. On the outside he felt he was acceptable, but on the inside, he felt like a jellyfish. He had not slept well — crying out loud for Constance, even getting up and walking through his bedroom corridor, screaming for his wife, but no answer came. He finally cried himself to sleep.

The crowd was huge — around three hundred people. His employees came out and stood behind him, some weren't smiling. Realizing their boss' behavior did not reflect well on the company. Charleton turned around and waved. All did not wave back. He looked to the right to see the General and to Charleton's surprise; Rose LaVon was standing next to him, looking as beautiful as ever. Neither of them looked happy or unhappy. To the left of them was his son, Ted, who smiled briefly — unsure of what his father was going to say.

Charleton looked down at his watch, cleared his throat and pursed his lips. He looked around once more wishing his wife was here. She had always gone with him before to every society function to be his support, but not today.

He cleared his throat again, rustled his speech papers that the General had given him a few weeks earlier. Looking down at them he began, "Uhmm, members of the press, friends, family and others, I come to you to formally ann…" just then he was interrupted by a man wearing jeans and a muscle t-shirt, with a long ponytail who began to shout, "Announce what! You beat your wife? It's funny, just because you have money to burn, that doesn't make you any better than the rest of us!" the heckler yelled, raising his hands in the air, causing others to raze Charleton too.

Charleton tried to ignore them by motioning them to just listen to what he had to say. He continued, "Sir, you're right — so very right. Folks, I came here today with a prepared speech I've been working on for weeks. Yes, I thought this would be a happy occasion announcing my intentions to be the best Governor this state has ever had. I thought I would talk about improving the revenue to debt ratio or how to improve the highways and schools. I thought I could help improve the tax structure, but in light of everything happening I feel I cannot serve the State of Missouri well enough right now."

"Yes, Salus Populi Suprema Lex Esto — our state motto (Let the welfare of the people shall be the supreme law). I feel inadequate at this time to live up to that."

"There's so much I really want to say. I wrestled all night with whether or not I should just read my speech and that's all. But, as I look into the crowd and see some people that through the years believed in me, people who thought I was a man who could do no wrong. I know I let them down big time and to my faithful employees, who helped me build my company, I should say our company. I'm sorry I let you all down. Most of all I let myself down and greater still I let my family down. I'm so tired of being a jellyfish in armor. I can't go on like this. I know I've been called a wife-beater by the press. Well, when I was arrested and jailed a few days ago, I began to really think about what I did to my wife Constance over the years. It was a criminal act and yes, I should have been locked up for what I did."

"I can't lie to you people anymore and I can't lie to myself anymore. I did abuse my wife physically and emotionally for which I am very, very sorry. I was a very foolish man. I am so horribly ashamed of myself. I stripped the one person I love more than anyone on this whole earth of her dignity. I was such a fool, such a fool."

"Folks, many of you have called me a monster, a label I hated from the first days I heard it and saw it in the newspapers, magazines, TV and radio, but now I must agree it is true. I am a monster."

"Yes, I know I won't change overnight, but I am willing to try and change through counseling and whatever else is necessary for me to be whole again. So, I want to announce to everyone here today and those who are watching and listening that I am officially withdrawing from the Governor's race, and I am also temporarily stepping down as CEO of Magenta Inc. I need some time to sort out my life."

"I'm a man and I'm made of clay too and I say to any man as well as to myself, never ever strike your wife. Please don't belittle her or call her stupid, because one day you may wake up and the love of your life is gone." Charleton said choking up when he saw people turning around whispering, as someone was slowly making their way through the crowd. From the platform he couldn't tell who this person was until they got closer. His jaw dropped when the person removed a large hat and sunglasses.

"Constance, you've come back! You've come back!" Charleton yelled as he started off the platform toward her. She stayed on the sidewalk, motioning for him to remain where he was. He did.

The press snapped picture after picture.

Constance spoke softly, "Charleton, I heard on the news you were going to go ahead with your speech, so I thought I'd say my little speech to you. Please don't interrupt me, and then I'll be gone."

"Last night, I finally made peace with God. I don't hate you anymore. I realize hating someone is really not the best thing to do. I asked God to let me have love for you again and I know it will take time."

"You really hurt me, Charleton. You broke my heart over and over again, so I began to search for answers, and I found them in the Bible. God's word says He can heal the brokenhearted and I'm convinced He can do that but first I have to give Him all the pieces, and I have. I realize I can be whole again; I need time away from you to sort out all that has happened to me."

"Charleton, you're such a brilliant man. Very few can stand up to you on that, but you never figured out what I needed, which just was so very, very simple. It's what every woman needs. They, we, need to be held and we need to be told that we are special and that we really and truly matter, and that we are the most important person in your life next to God."

"If you could have only figured out that a woman is like a beautiful flower, a beautiful rose that needs to be watered, cultivated and cared for daily or it will wither. Maybe things would have been different if you just paid a lot more attention to me, but I withered

Charleton. You were just too busy for me. I dried up. I no longer felt important in your life. I no longer felt needed."

"Will I come back? Only God knows, but for now this is goodbye to the only man I ever loved." Constance started to walk away but she saw her son walking toward her. They hugged and she whispered something in his ear.

After a long intense hug, Constance let go, kissed him on the cheek and started to walk back through the crowd. Charleton started to call her name and then stopped. He realized maybe it was best she did have her time alone. Then without warning, he remembered something he had heard in passing in the Atlanta airport years ago; "If true love was meant to be, set it free. If it comes back it was meant for thee."

Charleton closed his eyes, hoping to God that rhyme was really true.

www.ingramcontent.com/pod-product-compliance
Lightning Source LLC
Chambersburg PA
CBHW040423100526
44589CB00022B/2807